Out of the Fog
And Into the Light

An Addict's Journey to Self-Discovery

Sasha Skyy

Out of the Fog and Into the Light
Copyright © 2019 Sasha Skyy
ISBN: 978-1-970153-04-0

La Maison Publishing, Inc.

Maison
Vero Beach, Florida
The Hibiscus City

Dedication

I dedicate this book to all addicts and people struggling with mental illness and suicidal thoughts.

Dedication

I dedicate this book to all addicts and people struggling with mental illness and suicidal thoughts.

Acknowledgments

Mom - Without my mom and all of her help there is no way I could have finished this book. I call her "mom manager" for a reason.

Ellen - Thanks to Ellen's unique and one of a kind editing skills my book is a page turner. Thank you Ellen.

Janet - Thanks to Janet and all of her behind the scenes work, my book came out exactly how I wanted and is a beautiful finished book.

Velda - Thanks to my therapist for her ideas on certain topics to write about. This helped tremendously.

Lenny - Thank you for your beautiful photography work. Without your talent I would not have such a unique and magnificent cover.

Angels and spirit guides - Thank you for guiding me along. For standing beside me and behind me… giving me ideas and helping me push through the writer's block. Thanks for making this a healing experience rather than a painful one. I gratefully appreciate it.

Introduction

Imagine driving on a dark, foggy night, not really caring if you make it to your destination or not, because you have little hope you'll arrive. More and more often, you find yourself dwelling on sick thoughts, crazy thoughts, and dysfunctional thoughts. Life is overwhelming. The thought of not having to deal with it any more is increasingly appealing. You visualize smacking into a cement wall or driving into a deep ditch, knowing that there is no way in hell you would survive.

Or maybe you *would* survive, and then what?

Maybe this preoccupation with ending it all is just a cry for help, except no one can hear it. You're tired of faking it and putting on the happy face for everybody else's benefit when deep inside you're a train wreck. There doesn't seem to be a way out of the despair. You're stuck in a living, vicious nightmare in which you are constantly running from something. Awake, asleep, it doesn't really matter; the feeling of running, of trying to escape, haunts you all the time.

Finding yourself at a destination, arriving finally, discovering an escape route from your pursuer – these all seem like illusive miracles. Coming to the end of the nightmare and waking up to a beautiful day sounds like bliss itself. Without even knowing it at a conscious level, you *want* to get better and experience a joyous journey in this lifetime, not just hope for a better eternity. You *want* to have fun like the groups of friends you have observed laughing and having a good time together.

With the briefest hint of hope, however, comes the immediate awareness that this will never be your reality. You're not like those people. You have never fit in and you never will. You're "weird" or "different;" at least that's what others have whispered, or even said to your face, for as long as you can remember.

Welcome to my life! – or rather, the way my life was for a very long time. Can you imagine living like that? Then imagine this: you were not made for the fog and gloom. I was not, either. You were not destined for despair, just as I was not. You are a special person. You have unique gifts that cannot be understood by the same judgmental and materialistic people you think you should imitate. One day you'll understand. One day you will be content with who you are and who you have become. You can learn the things that I have learned.

I know what it is like to live in the fog, and I know what it is like to live in the light. Trust me, the light is better! I want to help you experience it, too – not only to step into the light, but to *stay* there.

Contents

Part 1: My Journey

Part 2: Healing

Trauma in Childhood

From a very young age, I was sensitive. As an infant and toddler, I cried so much that my mother didn't know what to do. She felt terrible leaving me, but she had a good full-time job, so good that she couldn't afford to lose it. She had to get back to work after I was born. Even though she would have loved to have been a stay-at-home mother, circumstances made that impossible. My father was unstable and never held a job for long. My mother couldn't rely on him for childcare, either, so she hired a nanny. It seemed like a good idea at the time.

It was not.

I don't remember the trauma that woman caused me, but it settled deep within my subconscious. The nanny used to lock me in the bedroom where I screamed in my crib. My mother would come home to find bruises on my arms from banging them against the crib, trying desperately to get out. When questioned, the nanny brushed it off. She patronized my mother, telling her that it was normal for a child my age. "All children fall down. They bump into things. It's nothing to worry about."

Time and distance have blurred the edges of memory. We are not quite sure how long this went on, but every day my mother came home and found more bruises and scrapes. Finally I screamed so loudly one day that the neighbors heard me. Through closed windows, they heard the terrifying sound of a terrified child. Thankfully, they did more than wonder about it; they investigated. When they discovered that I was locked in my room every day, crying and screaming until I fell asleep, exhausted, they were incredulous. *How does someone even do that? How cruel and disgusting must one be? How heartless!*

The neighbors contacted my mother at work, telling her to come home at once. The nanny was fired, of course, but beyond that, she was free to work elsewhere. Perhaps she was arrested at some point; perhaps not. I hope that she never traumatized another infant; perhaps she learned her lesson somewhere along the way and stepped out of her own fog, into her own light. I hope so.

I was not free, though. My mother tells me that long after the trauma ended, I would hit myself so hard that she had to hold me tightly, keeping my arms still as she rocked me.

Everything in our lives stems from childhood experiences. Every thought. Every feeling. Every emotion. My mother could keep me from hitting myself when I was a little girl, but I continued to abuse myself long after that. After an argument with my parents, I would run to my room and lock the door behind me; I hit myself, scratched myself, cut myself, banged my head against the wall. Sometimes one or two of those things, sometimes all of them. I always felt so alone, like no one cared about me, like I was still penned in by the slats of an invisible crib, locked inside a room, crying for help and getting no response.

My father had clinical depression, or at least we thought that was the problem. I was still fairly young when I realized that he was suffering from more than depression. It was heartbreaking and frightening. When I looked into eyes full of rage, he changed. It was as if he was not the same person.

3

It's hard to describe Other-Dad to anyone who hasn't seen such a transformation for themselves, but I compare it to an ex-boyfriend who was addicted to cocaine. He tried to overcome the addiction but during one relapse he went into what is called *cocaine psychosis*. He had something similar to one of my father's "episodes," during which he choked me inside a closet.

When he finally took his hands off me, I looked into his eyes and honestly had no idea whom I was looking at. I believe in angels and demons. You've heard of demonic activity? Well, this was as close to seeing a demon-possessed person that I ever wish to see. His eyes had startling black and dark purple circles around them. I wondered for a second if he even knew who I was anymore.

And in that moment, I wondered why cocaine was so much more important to him than I was, not understanding that it had nothing to do with me, that it was the addiction controlling him, not letting him think like normal people think. I literally ran for my life that night, hating him but at the same time still feeling great love for him in my heart. He was sick; he needed help.

How easy it is for us to question others with addictive behavior, while ignoring our own! I was struggling with drugs myself. But we'll look at that in a bit.

Back to my childhood – my father's behavior was much like bipolar disorder, sometimes called manic-depressive illness. That's why I didn't recognize him during an anger episode – something inside had shifted. He behaved like someone else, someone in pain, someone who wanted to cause pain to others. Thankfully, both my father and the ex-boyfriend are better now. They have gotten the help they needed. Their fogs have begun, at least, to lift.

My father's struggles began during his own childhood, perhaps, stemming from events he may have no remembrance of, just as I have no remembrance of the trauma I endured in my crib. Things happen. Bad things happen. If we ignore them, or pretend they didn't happen, the pain only continues.

My childhood was painful and difficult, even after the horrible nanny was no longer in my life. I was scared much of the time, because I felt like everything I did was wrong; nothing was ever good enough. I never knew what to expect from my dad. One day he was the greatest guy in the world,

5

in a good mood, having fun with me, talking to me and laughing with me like any loving father would do with his beloved daughter. Then out of nowhere, he would suddenly be angry at me for something minor.

I used to take snacks to school in Ziploc® baggies, for example. If I didn't bring them back home with me to be reused I might get screamed at. I never understood the rationale behind such things, the overreacting and the anger. These things led me to believe that everything I did was wrong.

We weren't poor. He simply wanted to reuse the bags. Nothing wrong with being thrifty, or reducing waste, but to let such things erupt in rage? How is a child equipped to see beyond the anger to the pain that causes it, pain that has nothing to do with Ziploc® bags or daughters?!

I remember these times, vividly. Those memories took root deep inside. I had let my father down. Disappointed him. Angered him. After it happened enough times, my feelings turned into anxiety and fear. I was petrified I would get yelled at, or worse. Because sometimes, he would be so angry that he pulled out the belt.

I don't believe that it is ever okay, under any circumstances, to hit a child, or to whip a child with a belt, or to discipline in anger. People try to justify it, but I don't buy it. "Well, he didn't hit you that hard." So that's okay then? My father was angry. He looked angry enough to kill me. How does a child understand that? Children who have been punished physically in anger, learn that violence is okay. They learn that *they are bad*. They learn to hate themselves because of all the wrong they've been told they've done. There are people who use discipline effectively, but I can guarantee you that they do not discipline with anger and violence.

Let me educate you on the way children think. If they want to show you something they made at school, but you yell at them because you're busy, you have taught them a negative lesson. Instead of communicating in a polite way that you're in the middle of something, and ask if it could wait just a minute – or better yet, you drop what you're doing to give your undivided attention – your reaction has taught these children that *they* have done something wrong. That they aren't good enough, that their very presence is an inconvenience. When this happens again and again, the

7

children are conditioned accordingly. Whenever the children are near you, they feel insecure. They should feel love and acceptance, but you have taught them that neither of these feelings is a reality.

This is the way children think. If a child thinks in this negative way often enough – or to put it another way, if the child is *taught* this often enough – it becomes a pattern or even a neuro-pathway in the brain. This child will think the thought ("I am bad") without even realizing it. The child grows up constantly receiving negative reinforcement, even inwardly. *Everything I do is wrong. I'm not good enough.* Unless damaged children are able to go back and alter traumatic memories in their subconscious, those memories remain, negatively affecting their lives in many ways.

But there is hope. I know this to be true, because of my own experience. Until I was able to alter those damaging memories in my subconscious, I was not able to heal. *And I am healed.*

Witnessing Suicide

One day when I was five years old, my mother and I had just returned to our house in Hauppauge, New York. My father wasn't inside as we expected, so we walked together into the garage to see if he was there. We found his car running in the closed garage. My father was inside the vehicle, trying to commit suicide by carbon monoxide poisoning. "Go back inside the house!" my mother directed me, following long enough to call a babysitter to watch me.

Even as a little girl, I had powerful intuition. My mother told me that my father had to go to the hospital because of kidney stones, but I knew it was something more serious than that. I didn't know exactly what had happened until much later in life, but I always knew it wasn't kidney stones!

I went to visit him in the hospital in a day or so, and he gave me a picture he had drawn. He was always talented in art; one of the things we enjoyed doing together was coloring and drawing. It was a simple picture, not one of his best because he had lacked materials, but for some reason I'll never forget it. It meant so much to me because I knew that deep inside he was suffering. I wasn't old enough to figure out why yet, but I could tell by his energy, by the expression on his face, by the way he slumped on the hospital bed, that he had gone through something serious. And for some reason, he felt ashamed about it.

When I walked into the garage with my mother and saw the car, heard the engine rumbling, smelled the fumes, found him drowsy inside ... I was only five years old. I didn't have the wisdom, intelligence, sophistication, or experience to draw accurate conclusions at the time, but it still affected me profoundly. My father was hurting, and he was embarrassed at having chosen the solution with the least possible chance of a positive outcome. And there wasn't anything I could do to help him.

I would eventually learn ... much, much later ... that in addition to other things, I am an *indigo child*. That explains a lot. For those who believe that humans are surrounded by energy fields of different colors which correspond to different gifts and personalities, indigo children emit that particular color. They are often seen as "strange" by others, even by family members. At that time, I was a hurting little girl, who knew things at a deeper level than most five-year-olds could connect to, but I also lacked the ability to act on those things. I lived inside the fog of negativity for so much of my formative years. Perhaps if I hadn't, however, I wouldn't appreciate the light as much as I do now.

Cool in School

I always felt awkward in school. The sense of not being *enough* and not being *good enough* spilled over from our family dynamics into every part of my life. In elementary school I could see who the popular girls were, but although I wanted to be friends with them, and although they accepted me to a certain extent, I still felt negative vibes, still felt their judgment.

Many years later, I was told that I am an *empath.* When this was explained to me, some of my past made more sense. The Greek word "pathos" means feeling, emotion, or suffering. When we are sympathetic, we care about the feelings of others; when we are *empathetic,* we feel it at a personal level, carrying it ourselves.

An empath is therefore dramatically affected by other peoples' energies. You can literally feel the energy of another person around you. Empaths are highly sensitive, which has both an upside and a downside. Empaths are there for you through thick and thin; we are naturally good listeners. We absorb other peoples' positivity, feeling every sensation and mood.

The downside? We absorb negativity as well. Empaths get exhausted being around negative energy. When we are around peace and love, our bodies flourish, but we do not live in a peaceful, loving world all of the time; reality can take a tremendous toll.

Many empaths are introverts, becoming overwhelmed in crowds. For example, when I go to the supermarket, or any place where there are lots of people, I sometimes have to put a shield up, literally, because of the draining power of all that energy flowing around me. Because of this tendency, empaths prefer one-on-one contact or being among small groups. When we get drained from being around a lot of energy, we need alone time to "recharge."

Empaths are also highly intuitive. We have learned from experience to listen to our gut feelings about people and situations. If we have the choice, we prefer taking our own car, rather than riding with a friend, so that we can leave when we need to. That may seem odd to others, especially when many folks like to save gas and money by carpooling, but empaths learn to protect themselves in such ways.

We can become overwhelmed in intimate relationships. Think about this. The energy of complete strangers can affect us – how much more, the energy of those closest to us? An empath may fear losing his or her identity, feeling so much of what another is feeling, that it becomes entangled with one's own.

Relationships, intimate or surface, need to be simple for us empaths. No drama. Empaths are targets for energy vampires, life drainers, and narcissists who suck the energy out of a room, making everything only about what they want and think and need.

Nature acts as a healing balm for empaths, which I'll go into in more detail in Part Two. The busyness of everyday life can be too much for us. Like some on the autism spectrum, our senses may be highly tuned; we can get frazzled by loud noises, smells, or incessant talking. Nature's antidote can sooth all of that away. Being surrounded by relaxing greenery, or sitting at the ocean's shore as the waves ebb and flow, the sound of their crashes, the birds interrupting occasionally. Everyone can benefit from nature's relaxation therapy, but empaths must have it, or suffer.

When I was told that I was an empath, much of my past made more sense. Those girls in elementary school felt judged, and so I felt it, too, when I was around them. At the time, it was hurtful and baffling. As I got a little older, unfortunately, things did not improve.

We moved to Florida when I was still in elementary school, but my first real boyfriend didn't come on the scene until I was in the seventh grade. I thought to myself, with all the maturity I felt, "This is it. This is love." Two months of this young "love," and I was gearing up mentally and emotionally for a proposal! Instead, he dumped me.

Why? Who knows. There probably wasn't even a reason other than the fact that we were both children, still unformed. I cried and cried. I cried for *days*. Looking back, I appreciate how ridiculous it was, but it felt like a completely appropriate response to the End of My Life.

I began drinking around this time, at the age of twelve. What began as somewhat innocent experimentation became a weekend ritual. I thought it was what most teens did, and I desperately wanted to be like "most teens," struggling as I was, feeling different and inadequate. From the novelty of light-headedness to the silliness of getting tipsy, why not spend every weekend with best friends getting wasted? Every broken heart added an excuse to drink more.

Middle school romance is a fairly hilarious concept when you think about it. You fall in and out of love; you're barely into puberty. You date someone for a few weeks and barely know each other. The inevitable, tragic ending is painful. But you keep doing it, because those butterflies in the stomach are so exciting when you pass Mr. Wonderful a note in the hallway or kiss him for the first time. Then you meet someone MORE wonderful, with whom you share more in common. Time for "the talk," the breaking up, the breaking hearts, the freedom now to stalk new prey. At least kids that age are pretty straightforward, telling it like it is, instead of the cheating and lying we all too often deal with as adults.

School was not all butterflies and breakups, however. It amazes me that I not only made the effort to try out for cheerleading, but I also made the squad! I was a "flier," enjoying the weightless feeling when others would throw me up in the air during a routine.

I enjoyed it right up until I got dropped on my head. I thought my brain was broken! It might be in the fog most of the time, but it wasn't broken. Used to feeling alone and on the "outs," I gobbled up the attention from my parents and classmates until it became apparent that I was fine.

Real tragedy did appear in my teen years, but not in a way that affected me directly. It never fails to depress me now, however, when I think about the night I lost four classmates involved in a major car accident. One of my friends was the driver who, with three other students (including a boy I'd developed quite a crush on), decided to go on a "joy ride" late at night. The night ended as anything but joyful.

Even students who were not close to them, who were not naturally empathetic, had a difficult time. Teenagers think they're immortal, that they have so much time ahead of them. It was a stark reminder to us all, but perhaps because I dealt with the constant pressure of feelings on a daily basis, the accident was a particularly dramatic blow to me. Such a loss.

One seemingly innocuous decision, and four families changed forever, with many other lives affected deeply.

High school is challenging under the best of circumstances, but for me, it was extremely difficult. I struggled with what had been diagnosed as intense ADHD – Attention-Deficit/Hyperactivity Disorder. I mentioned that I was an "indigo child" earlier. I believe that many indigo children are misdiagnosed with ADHD. We operate at a different level, one that imposed structures such as classrooms are not equipped to handle. At the time, I was regarded as a problem child who *had* problems. Much later, when I was told of indigo children, my childhood suddenly made sense.

So I had a hard time fitting in. I never felt comfortable. I was always paranoid. When someone labeled me as "weird" – it happened fairly often – I had to agree. I *was* weird, only my definition of the word is now *freaking awesome*! Heightened senses and this supersonic intuition no one could explain made me seem strange at the time, someone to steer clear of, maybe even be a little afraid of. Haters gonna hate, as they say, but mostly they are fearful.

I didn't even realize what it all meant myself, so how could they? Now that I understand that I have been blessed with spiritual gifts for a higher purpose, I see my life as a blessing. I am, and will always be, grateful that I was the "weird" one.

Like the typical indigo, I wondered when in the *hell* I would ever use the crap I was required to learn in school, what in the hell it was for, why in the hell I was there! I was bored out of my mind and had figured out long ago that I was not destined for college. I was sure that college would only be more of the same crap. No thank you.

I may have been weird in school, but I was also a party girl. Sneaking out of my garage window, I'd get picked up to go to a party or just go out drinking. Somehow I stumbled back through the window and made it to school later that morning. This amazes me, looking back. How did I manage all that subterfuge while completely smashed? Today, I would be falling on my face!

My best friend Megan had the best "window" to sneak out of. We basically could just waltz out the door of her house, and waltz (albeit in a stupor) back in. We had some good times, or what we thought were good times – until the night we got caught.

For years, I had had thoughts, premonitions, feelings that something might happen. But that day was the first time I knew something bad was going to happen. *I knew it*, and still I plunged ahead. Frankly, the element of impending disaster made it even more delicious.

When Mom's number popped up on my cell phone at around 4:30 am, I knew I was busted. We had a trip planned for Hilton Head, Mom's favorite vacation spot. We were supposed to go with her friend, and now this. No trip today! Mom was sure that I'd never make that mistake again, but to me, since the worst had already happened, why not just keep doing it?

During high school I was still being verbally abused by my father. Sometimes, I was physically abused, but only slightly – a smack on the head in passing, a rough grab of my arm. Nothing major. Nothing reportable. Nothing worth risking an escalation or a divorce.

But one Christmas Eve, for most folks one of the cheeriest nights of the year, I was making food in the kitchen when my father came in yelling. Out of nowhere, after a pleasant, uneventful day, he was angry that I was eating! I was no longer a timid toddler, however. I had learned to argue back, and argue I did.

Then he grabbed the dog leash. I dropped the bowl I was holding and ran as fast as I could back to my room. My father was at my heels, chasing me with a damn dog leash. Physically fighting him off, I managed to shut my door with me on the inside and him still yelling in the hallway. I just stood there, listening, unable to make sense of his anger, screaming hysterically as he banged on my door.

"Open this door or else!" he kept saying. *Or else what?* If I opened the door, I would get beaten with a dog leash, which didn't seem like a good option.

My mother had joined him by this time; I could hear her trying to calm him down. "Get away from him!" I shouted. "He'll hurt you!"

Mom was brave, though, and I think she knew that he wouldn't hit her. Oddly, I was always the target of his anger, not Mom. Her presence had some effect, anyway, because he ran to his room and pushed his dresser in front of the door so we couldn't get in. Now that the tables were turned – he was inside a locked door, and we were free – he went into

21

Sasha Skyy

bathroom and swallowed all the pills he found in the medicine cabinet.

Somehow we pried open the door and found him lying on the floor, motionless. The smell of the garage that day when I was five washed over me. He had tried this before. Now I understood.

Mom called 9-1-1; an ambulance came and left. The next morning was Christmas, but it didn't feel like Christmas, not after the Christmas Eve we had suffered. I couldn't stop crying. For years I had begged my mom to divorce my dad. Now all I could think of was, "I don't want my father to die."

My mom and dad did separate after that incident and divorced a few years later. He stayed in my life but not on any regular basis. When we saw each other our relationship did not improve. Over the years I had grown accustomed to the one element of consistency about my father: his *inconsistency*. I was used to the abuse and the trauma, but the thought of not having a father figure in my life – abusive of not – just killed me. The truth of the matter was that he had never been a real father figure. Because of his influence in my life, I had tons of trauma, baggage, flashbacks all the time. His death would have meant a quieter, more stable life for me –

but it would have also meant more baggage. My last memory of him would have been Christmas Eve.

Some of this, I felt at the time. Other parts, I came to understand over time.

Don't get me wrong, my father was wonderful at times. At times. But when the rage came over him, it was frightening. I hated that we fought so much. And I always wondered why my mother never stood up for me – this laid the groundwork for serious relationship issues that we, happily, came to resolve, but that would be years down the road (and pages further in this book!).

Mom tried to calm us both down, staying in the middle without taking my side against him. Today, she regrets that she didn't do more to protect me. I was only a child when the rages began, and they never were far away for long. Parents are supposed to guide and protect you until you're able to be stable on your own. I had a very different experience with both my mother and father when I was young.

I believe in reincarnation. You may not, but knowing why I do may help you understand my thinking, and by extension, help you understand your own. I believe that before children are born, their spirits are in and out of their mothers' wombs.

A child chooses her parents based on what will expand her consciousness the most, what will be the best learning experience for her. She chooses the parents she wants for her new incarnation. Inside the womb, the child may remember her past life entirely or be completely disconnected from what has taken place beforehand.

There is behind-the-scenes planning, pre-birth planning. Many children remember choosing their parents after birth. We're given many choices before we are born: Some choose the easy way, the path of least resistance. Others prefer maximum growth in order to take care of major, or many lifetimes, of karma.

Apparently, I chose a very rough ride! Despite this, I would not trade it for anything. Everything I endured as a child enabled me to reach this incredible cosmic moment where all is understood.

Science and medicine tell us that pollutants such as substances found in processed food in the United States or certain medications can tremendously affect childbirth. Even more important, however, is the way children are raised. That is the main factor of any child's spiritual awareness and essence.

I was a free spirit from the beginning. I spent most of my childhood outside, going on journeys and adventures, feeling connected to Mother Nature in an indescribable way. I remember spinning in circles, something I like to do to this day, connecting with the ground below as well as with the central sun above. As a child, I was amazed by the feel of the breeze on my skin, the smell of fresh air. Inspecting dandelions assured me that this life was greater and more expansive than I knew, even as I dealt with the often troubling situations at home or school.

I've always had the ability to communicate on an unusual level with birds generally, and ducks, specifically. All cultures embrace the idea of particular animals that guide and protect individuals. Ducks are indeed some of my power animals; the way that I connect with them even today is incredible to me. I will talk more about that later.

As a child, I loved climbing trees. With typical indigo child independence, I constantly pushed the outside of the envelope, climbing higher than my parents permitted. A little higher than was okay, a little further than my given boundaries of exploration – only then did I feel truly connected to the world. For some reason I never understood,

I filled my wagon with acorns and lugged them home. Perhaps the squirrel is one of my power animals as well!

I was always a loner as a youngster. I had friends, but their preferred play activities bored me. Toys? Dolls? Where was the fun there? I used to rip the heads off of Barbie dolls, attempting to flush them down the toilet just to see what would happen. I wanted to explore anything and everything.

At one point, I sincerely believed that I was Indian. I asked Mom to braid my hair every morning into two long braids. I wore moccasins instead of sneakers. Instead of pastels and primary colors from Oshkosh B'Gosh® like most of my friends wore, I tried my best to look like a Native American - despite being pale, with blonde hair and blue eyes.

That may not have been a childhood phase, however. When we went to Arizona and peered into the Grand Canyon I experienced such a profound sense of familiarity, it is easy for me to believe that perhaps, in a former life, I was a Native American, or even a shaman of some sort.

Partying takes Over

By the age of sixteen, I spent more time away from the comfort and wonderment of nature, and more time tripping inwardly. I tried all the hardcore drugs: cocaine, ecstasy, whatever I could get. Because of my ADHD, coke gave me a different experience than what I observed in my friends. I always wondered what it was *supposed* to do. So I would do more and more of it to try to figure it out for myself. *What is it that coke is* supposed *to do? What is this high* supposed *to feel like?* I took so many drugs that one night that I ended up in the hospital. Despite feeling that this was the end, I survived, and didn't learn a thing.

When I got addicted to ecstasy, I *had* to do it. Once you're hooked, there is no longer a choice. *Every* weekend. Ecstasy landed me in the hospital, too. The story I told my mother was that my drink must have been spiked at some party I was at in the woods. She believed me, because she wanted to believe me.

Another hospital stay might have slowed down a lot of folks, but not *this* indigo! I was doing a line the next weekend. I had my first real boyfriend to speak of, but addiction is a strict master. I only really cared about partying. Despite this, I decided that I was in love with that young man at about the same point he cheated on me. I felt as if I was stabbed in the heart with a sword. All trust was broken, not only with him but for every man in my future. Bear in mind, I was still a teenager, still immature and unformed, carrying around an increasingly heavy load of baggage, living in an increasingly dense fog.

One time I was drunk at a particular party. I was still a virgin at the time. There was a guy there who was super hot, one of the most popular guys there. All the girls wanted to hook up with him, including me. Somehow I ended up outside with him, which at first was a very cool thing. We started kissing, and his hands were soon everywhere. I was quite pleased with the way things were going until suddenly, he began performing oral sex on me. I had heard the term "going down on" by then, but I had no idea what to do or what it was supposed to feel like. Because I wanted to impress him, I acted like I was enjoying it. I was not. Once again, the sensation of being trapped, stuck, behind bars was powerful.

It only got worse from there. After a few minutes, he whipped out his penis. From what I remember, he was huge – at least he looked huge to me! Because I was a virgin, I was very tight down there; when he tried to penetrate me, it hurt! I screamed and pushed against him but he held me down, still attempting to rape me.

"What the hell do you think you're doing!" I yelled. He was a big guy, but I somehow shoved him off of me and ran, panting for air. When I found my friends, I said nothing about what had happened. I was ashamed and embarrassed. The fog grew thicker and darker as I held the trauma of that night in for years. I was so afraid that night, that I've often wondered if that had something to do with my sexual identity – such questions would come much later.

Some students spread a nasty rumor about me the summer after my sophomore year, so nasty that I switched schools. Given my *actual* lifestyle at the time, you know the rumor had to be bad! I began attending an adult high school where students progressed at their own pace. My best friend Amy enrolled too, and I took her with me every day. We were practically connected at the hip, others teased.

One night, out of the blue, Amy texted me something unusual, completely unlike her: "Be safe tonight." Soon after she sent it, unbeknownst to me, she got into a dune buggy with her boyfriend and another couple. While crossing a road, they were hit by a drunk driver. Amy was the only one who did not survive.

Looking back, I'd have to say that this was one of the hardest times in my life. Amy held such a special place in my heart. She was loving and caring, generous and nonjudgmental. We were, in so many ways, alike. For me (the weird girl) to find a kindred spirit, was gold and Amy was my little nugget to love. I loved her so very much. For the next two months, I spent most of my time at her house, day and night, breathing her in, holding her possessions. School was forgotten. Heartbroken, I became super close to Amy's mother, who didn't mind me hanging out there at all.

When I got to know Amy's other best friend, Shawna, things got better. She was another genuinely good person. No wonder she was Amy's friend! I started back to school; Shawna and I rode with each other. I graduated from high school, but I was far from being ready to face the world as an adult.

I had known that college wasn't for me, but I couldn't just sit around. I began modeling, and eventually got quite a bit of work in Miami. Model... party... model... party. That was my life. From the outside, it may have seemed like someone's ideal, but inside the fog, it was far from it.

One weekend I was modeling in Miami and went to a club there. It's expensive to live in Miami, but I commuted, so I had saved a lot. I had tons of clothes, CDs, and money in my car, but I never worried about it. I was usually one of the last clubbers to leave. Because the clubs I frequented were opened for after-hours, it wasn't late at night when I left, it was early in the *morning*, well after the sun was up.

I'd gone to the club with a friend, and that morning, we walked out together, heading for my car. Except that it wasn't there. My first thought was that it had been towed, but no. It had been stolen. My Honda Civic was, at the time, the most stolen car in America, something the salesman hadn't thought to mention!

The club's DJ was nice enough to give us cab money to my friend's house, where I filed a police report. Amazingly, officers found the car the very next day, stripped and robbed of every item. That is the *modus operandi* for the homeless, apparently: Find a car that's easy to steal, strip it, and then abandon it. *What a life* – then again, you will learn things about me that will likely have you saying the same thing.

Oddly, I was the most upset over losing the CDs. My car was drive-able, but when I took it in for repair, the prognosis was bleak. It would take weeks to fix. I ended up getting a new car and selling the Civic when it was repaired.

When I was nineteen, I moved to Miami with the idea of modeling more, but unfortunately, the pull toward partying was stronger. I had also developed an eating disorder. As a model, I needed to look terrific at all times, right? That thought consumed me, controlling whether I left my apartment or not.

During the week, I stayed in my room unless my makeup was perfect and I was skinny enough. If not, I isolated myself. Those old lies and thought patterns from childhood had never left me: *You're not good enough. You'll never succeed. You're a disappointment.* Now they translated into "you're too fat." The fog swirled ominously. Light was getting harder and harder to find, even in small doses.

On weekends, though, I partied, scales and fog be damned. I'd go to Club Nocturnal on Fridays, an after-hours club, arriving around ten at night, hobbling out after the sun came up. My feet would hurt from dancing fourteen hours straight. I literally danced the night away.

Hurting feet didn't stop me from going to Club Space every *Saturday* night, though. Once again, I would get there at ten pm and stay until the club closed after sunrise. This was my routine, religiously adhered to. Sometimes I would go to after-hours down the street before catching a little sleep... so that I could go out again later.

Sundays belonged to Nikki Beach, my favorite. It was right on the beach; the DJ started outside and moved inside at around eight. It was hopping all night long, open until six the next morning, after which I might go to after-hours at another club, and then another. Once I started, the partying often leeched into Monday or even Tuesday. Who needed a gym when I could dance all night, all day, all weekend long?

After the first year, I moved into a place with a woman named Marie. In love with me, she considered me her girlfriend. I was pretty sure I was straight, but I had to admit that I liked the idea of living with her. I liked the fact that she liked me. At some level I must have known but not really "known" at that age about my sexuality, but I certainly wasn't ready to come out of the closet.

Marie would have done anything for me but her devotion went beyond affection, beyond love. She was obsessed. And I was confused. While I figured out who I really was and what I really wanted, I led her on. Living in the fog, that kind of thing becomes the norm.

I picked up some part-time office work for a web producer in South Beach and partied on the weekends. Not much changed, despite Marie and my confusion. I was the poster child for "party animal." The music, the sound, everything about it was so good, I couldn't get enough. The thumping of the bass brought chills down my spine and a huge smile upon my face. Dancing for 14 hours straight? That was my thing. I danced with guys, I danced with girls. Marie and I started having issues. Unable to deal with her jealousy, I moved out, jumping from the proverbial frying pan into the fire.

Living with Marie, beginning to come to grips with the fact that I was gay or I *might* be gay, was a crazy time. When we split up, life got even crazier. Who moves in with someone they picked up at a train station? Those who are blinded by the fog, that's who!

Lauren had five dollars to her name when we met, because she had spent the rest of her money on a down payment for a place in SoBe, what we called South Beach. My mother, who I told I needed to live in Miami for my modeling, kindly lent me a thousand dollars so we could move in. One bedroom. We led a crazy life, going from party to party, nonstop, after-hours to after-hours. It's a wonder we lived long enough to tell the tale.

We didn't live *together* for long, though. Lauren met a guy on the street with whom she promptly fell in love. She moved in with him, leaving me with an apartment lease I couldn't afford. I couldn't even pay my half of the rent without my mom's help; how was I supposed to afford it *all*?

As I mentioned, my mom thought I was looking for modeling jobs and working part time. I was able to fake my behavior when she was around, and she was naive to the party life, so she really thought she was helping me, rather than enabling me to continue a destructive lifestyle.

Modeling was out of the picture – so much for a promising career. Partying just about everyday plays havoc with your looks. Drinking. Drugging. I took a lot of ecstasy, and now I tried roxies (roxicodone) with my neighbor. To give you an idea of what a wonderful influence he was on me, I spent half the time picking him up from jail, and the other half getting high with him.

My feelings ran deep for him, however. I wanted him to be my boyfriend – the feeling was, alas, not mutual. He used me for rides home and to get laid. For a girl who grew up thinking she wasn't good enough, the arrangement was logical in its own way. I was good enough for *that*.

Finances were a major issue, though. While most men considered me to be charming, landlords were another matter. I met an older man with a large house and a roommate, also an older man. Amazingly, he invited me to stay with no strings attached. When I went to see the house, I was surprised to learn that his roommate was a man I'd known before, a man who had made it clear he was attracted to me.

I put a lot of stock in synchronicity. Things do not happen by accident. There is always a reason. Knowing the roommate before, meeting the older man, visiting the house, being invited to stay – all of these separate events meshed together. And too, I just really needed a place to live! A huge house with an incredible pool worked nicely. Living with two older guys, one of whom thought he might be in love with me, well, that was something I'd deal with eventually. My lifestyle had conditioned me to live for the moment, and at the moment, it all looked good.

It became fairly obvious that the men wanted a hot girl to prance around the house, but that wasn't who I wanted to be. I may have been a party girl and an addict, but deep down, I knew I couldn't be happy under those conditions. It was hard on me. I liked the guy who wanted me to be his girlfriend, but there were no sparks between us, at least from my perspective.

Time marched on. I met a Brazilian man named Dan that I clicked with immediately. Increasingly, I spent the night with him, an arrangement that didn't sit well with the two older guys. Without a boyfriend in the picture, they could control me much more easily, keep me all to themselves, and perhaps plan for a future romance. With a boyfriend ... they kicked me out.

Which was why, much too quickly in a new relationship, I moved in with Dan. At first, it was great. Marie, Lauren, everyone else – all forgotten. *This was love*. Finally feeling a bit of normalcy creeping into my life, I no longer wanted to party as much. I had a reason to settle down, to relax at home with this man I adored.

Dan, however, wanted the complete opposite. That isn't to say that I was right and he was wrong – everyone lives his own life and has his own unique journey. But our relationship eventually developed problems that went beyond a conflict about what we'd do that evening. It became abusive. It became toxic.

I understand now that our relationship mirrored the abusive, toxic relationship I had with myself, but I couldn't see that in the fog. I had started to abuse my own flesh again. I didn't love myself. I treated myself horribly at times. Eventually, I became so jealous and insecure towards Dan that I could no longer handle having a boyfriend who did exactly what I had done when we met – party all the time.

Leaving him hurt deeply, because I loved him. But I also knew I had to get out.

Ron, a gay male friend, said I could sleep on his couch. Sometimes, I slept in his bed. This did nothing to clear up my confusion regarding my own sexuality! With my past, I could accept the fact that I was bisexual, but still I wondered if I was, in reality, a full-blown lesbian.

It would have taken too much energy to find out, however, by this time, I was an addict through and through. Sex – whether with a man or a woman – wasn't my priority, only drugs. Roxies were my drug of choice. I crushed the pills and sniffed the substance, getting it into my system more quickly. I had started using roxies with Dan, but when I moved out, the addiction got worse.

My friend Ron was nice enough to let me stay, but I wasn't very good company. I was heartbroken, struggling to get over Dan. I was determined not to slip backward, however. What was I moving toward? I had no idea. But I would not, could not go back.

Not to make an excuse, but my job as a call girl, to put it mildly, was a factor in my decision making at the time. I wasn't a stripper, not that there's anything wrong with that.

People need to make ends meet, and sometimes we "gotta do what we gotta do." No one should point fingers when we're all just trying to survive, but I have to point the finger at myself for this one. I feel great shame writing about it, a personal low point.

Sleazy guys came in to the place I worked, technically for a massage. Everyone knew the real reason they were there. I have no idea if this period in my life also played into me being gay, having no attraction towards men, but it very well may have.

Worse, at least in my thinking, the men who came in were mostly married. I don't know how anyone could do that to his own wife – and they were doing it with *me*, a random girl they didn't know. It made me feel like men don't give a shit about anyone but themselves, that they just do whatever they want without even thinking about it. I kept thinking that they were just animals. And then I would think about the fact that they were committing these degrading and vile acts with me. If they were animals, what did that make me?

Even though I feel so much shame writing this, maybe there is someone out there who needs to read this, who can relate. I prostituted myself for the money, so much money –

and I needed every penny to support my drug habit. It was a destructive, vicious cycle: I had to do drugs in order to get through a job that disgusted me, and I needed the job to buy the drugs. It all went hand in hand.

Deep down, beyond the lies and the fog, there was a whisper that I deserved better, a glimmer of light, but at the time I was deaf. I was blind. I didn't know what "better" was. As difficult as the "massage" work was, I couldn't see an alternative. I had to make money, and this was the only way.

When I saved up a little money, I left Ron's and rented from my boss at the time. He needed all the rooms in his house, so I slept on an air mattress in the living room. It was pretty sad. I desperately needed my own place, but I was also using heavily, up to twenty *roxies* a day. Drugs, in case you didn't know this, are a costly habit.

I didn't realize, of course, how severe my problem was at the time. I had no clue that I would have to go through an arduous detoxification process just to get off the bullshit. Years later, it's still difficult for me to believe how much money and energy I wasted on those suckers just to get high! And to make matters worse, after a while I didn't even *get* high. But still I used. That was my life. I had to.

Period Issues

Ever since puberty, I've suffered with PMDD, Pre-Menstrual Dysphoric Disorder. It was horrible. Two full weeks of every month, I was confined to bed, suffering from pain, chronic fatigue, and major depression. Sometimes I just lay there crying, sometimes I was suicidal. This also meant that half of every month my isolation negatively affected all of my relationships, friendships, and jobs.

No one had an answer for me. I even went going on birth control, but everything I tried made me gain weight. My eating disorder wouldn't put up with *that*. Birth control pills also made me even more suicidal. Trying to combat the depression that was linked to the PMDD, I tried prescriptions from a psychiatrist which also did not work. Again the suicidal thoughts increased. I had always been emotionally dysfunctional and behaviorally dysfunctional. Wasn't that what everyone thought? What I heard from everyone? Now I was hormonally dysfunctional too. When I cried for two weeks every month, I was actually crying out for help. Couldn't anyone hear me?

Jail and Beyond

Finances in a nosedive, hormones in a tizzy, addiction, eating disorder, baggage, failed relationships, mental lies – all of it swirled inside that fucking fog in my brain. Life was complicated enough already when I met Andre, by far the craziest dude I've known and the craziest relationship I've ever been in. *All* he cared about was where the next party was and getting, as he put it, "fucked up." I don't know why or how I fell for him, but I fell hard. Still addicted to drugs but away from what I had thought I might have with Dan, I was going out more and more. I lived to party; Andre lived to party. It was a match made ... well, not in heaven, but you get the idea.

After a while Andre and I moved into our own place. Sort of. We shared the house with another couple, but it was usually filled to the brim with people because it was The Party House. Andre sold drugs out of the house during parties, confident that he would get away with it.

What we didn't count on was the fact that we were being watched by undercover cops.

Our relationship was shitty, too. He was always mad at me, abusive in every way a man can be abusive. And I just took it. There were moments of happiness, but *only* moments. The emotional roller coaster was nothing short of brutal. Andre would go out without me ... again ... and leave me hanging. Then he would apologize and all was forgiven and forgotten. Until it happened again.

I was twenty-three when we both went to jail. Andre was arrested when he sold drugs to an undercover cop. During their search, cops found pills in my purse and told me they would help me if I cooperated. Their help" was not what I expected – detoxing in a jail cell was the worst experience of my life, so far. Jail was *cold*. Everything about it was horrible. It would have been awful under the best of circumstances, but detoxing made me miserably sick.

It may sound strange, but I honestly had no idea that getting off drugs would send every fiber of my being into a spiral. Detoxing from that shit was indescribably bad. *Wow, I thought in the middle of another spasm of vomiting. What an experience. If I'd known then it would do this, would I have started? Is* anything *worth this?* Detoxing won't kill you, but you wish that it would.

The hell, in this case, lasted only a few days. My parents bailed me out, paying my $75,000 bond on top of the lawyer's fees. They were financially comfortable, but not so comfortable that my bond didn't put a dent in their account. A *big* dent.

The wheels of justice, I learned, do not turn quickly. It was three years before I went to court, during which time I went through five or six treatment centers, none of *them* cheap either, not to mention the halfway houses after them. What a waste, not only of money but also of time and energy.

The first treatment center I went to turned out to be for people who just kept relapsing so it was a little advanced for me. I was on the wrong meds at the time and if you know me you know I need to be on adderall or ritalin or *something*, or I fall asleep everywhere and generally act like a goofball. I know they're narcotics but some people legitimately need to be on them. I also have serious chronic fatigue and if you don't have it, you have no idea what it feels like. Tired all of the damn time. Falling asleep literally anywhere.

I got in a lot of trouble at that first treatment center. I talked too much and apparently got flirted with too much by the many guys that were at the center with me. There was a lot of drama, always. When the girl in the room next to me went to the doctor one day, she literally drank all of the hand sanitizer in the office. She got a hold of mouthwash and drank a whole bottle. And *then* her alcoholic ass got my hairspray and drank all of that because we had conjoined bathrooms. It was interesting, to say the least. Her breath was fresh, but her actions were not okay! Looking back sober, it's hard to imagine how far people will go to get the next drink or drug – how far *I* would go. The mouthwash girl ended up in the hospital, by the way, and eventually got sober.

My second treatment center was more of like a transitional living type place. It was a huge, beautiful house, but trying to deal without the correct meds was just as horrible. I had a spectacular room all to myself. I met an awesome girl and we quickly became close friends. At first, I did everything right. I even got a job, at a hair salon.

Unfortunately, it didn't take long for my stupidity and the other girl's stupidity to kick in.

We decided someone's birthday was the perfect excuse to do "whip its," where we sucked the air out of the whipped cream container to get high. It was a terrible idea; a month or so later when a staff person found a bottle of whipped cream in the refrigerator, someone told on us and we both got kicked out.

I had a job. I was going to meetings. I was doing so well – wasn't the "whip it" ancient history anyway, a month later? I was sent to a third treatment center.

Whereas the huge house had been relaxing, this place was fast paced, go-go-go. They had us doing things from the moment we woke up until the moment we went to bed. It was too much for me. I need breaks and rest. I was very tired as usual; once again I fell asleep often and get yelled at during groups. They didn't understand that I couldn't control it, that chronic fatigue wasn't related to my addiction. Also, this center was super expensive – I was only there until I could get a bed in something more affordable.

The fourth treatment center I went to was called Wayside. The plan was to eventually get phased out into a halfway house; I could work. That was the plan.

Let me just say that I hate treatment centers. Not knowing anyone when you first get there is the worst; I felt so alone. I was still super tired, constantly taking naps or falling asleep during groups. It took a while, but I finally made good friends there. Family was able to visit on weekends; we had family groups. I used to beg my mom and dad to let me leave with them. I hated being tired all the time; I hated that the powers-that-be wouldn't let me take my medication. They distributed the meds, so it's not like I could abuse them. Some people legitimately need narcotics to function, and I'm one of them. I guess they'd been burned enough that they thought they knew it all, but that wasn't the way I saw it.

We went to meetings every day. After "graduation," we were supposed to find jobs, but I could not find one. Anywhere. After a few months with no job on the horizon, I guess they didn't know what to do with me anymore; next stop? A halfway house. That actually went well enough that I was able to get an apartment. And a boyfriend.

True Love Enters My Life

When I got out of treatment, I found the real love of my life. Not a boyfriend. Not a girlfriend! My dog Skyy came into my life unexpectedly. Ross was my boyfriend at the time; he and I discussed wanting a dog. But we weren't really looking for a dog when Skyy showed up out of nowhere.

Skyy was a rescue. A friend had found her in the middle of the road, taking her home. She called all the animal shelters, looked around for signs – *Missing, The Perfect Dog* – but she wasn't having any luck. One day when she met me at a kava bar, she brought the dog with her. I was drawn to her like a magnet, staring into this magnificent pup's eyes. It was truly love at first sight.

Skyy didn't have the same reaction at first. She was scared and shy, backing away a little when I tried to pet her. I could tell she hadn't been treated right. She was sort of beaten up looking. But she was the most beautiful creature I had ever seen with big hazel eyes, a slick black coat, and the cutest ears I'd ever seen on a dog.

My friend said there were people lining up to take her, which was disappointing. I said, "Well, if you can't find a home for her, I want her."

Back at home, I told my boyfriend about the wonderful puppy I had seen. He wasn't sure, and anyway, someone else had probably already taken her. A few days later, however, my friend said she wanted me to have the dog. I was ecstatic. I knew Ross would go crazy when he saw her, and I was right – how could anyone resist a dog that cute?

I named her Skyy with two y's because I always had to be unique, ya know! From the beginning, she has been an angel, going through many trials and tribulations at my side. When Ross and I broke up, he kept her for a while because I couldn't have dogs where I lived, but I quickly discovered that I couldn't be without her – better to change my living arrangements than to lose Skyy!

Skyy watched me go through my addiction. I could tell she was disappointed when I used drugs; I could read her like a book then, and I can read her like a book now. She reads me just as well! I mentioned earlier about an ex-boyfriend who choked me. That was Ross. When it happened, Skyy barked throughout the ordeal, not knowing what to do but sticking with me nevertheless. After that incident, I ran with her, got her into the car, and got the hell away.

Skyy and I are connected; our souls mesh. She's my partner in crime and I'd do anything for her. She, in turn, comforts me and is always by my side. I have no idea who in the past could have hurt this sweet little thing, but their loss was definitely my gain.

Even after all the treatment centers and halfway houses, I drifted back into addiction. At one point, detoxing from twenty Dilaudids® a day, Skyy stubbornly stayed by my side. I couldn't get up for three days to take her out. I *wanted* her to go to the bathroom in the house, because I knew I couldn't take care of her, but she refused. During those three days, still unable to walk, I managed to get her out now and then by crawling to the door. She still stayed by my side. There is no other way to describe Skyy except as an angel just dropped from heaven. A lot of dogs sleep on their owner's bed, but Skyy has to be physically touching me. She sleeps under the covers with me! It's the cutest thing, but it also reinforces our bond. It also comforts both of us with the power of touch.

My Skyy is the chillest, most laid back, most loving dog on the planet. What more could a person want? I am truly blessed, and truly in love.

The Fog Settles Back In

Even though I had Skyy after I got out of treatment, I still didn't have a full recovery yet. After a half-way house and while dating Ross, I moved in with a roommate. I started using a little bit here and there, nothing major, nowhere near the amount I had been into, so I felt like I was "behaving." The people I was hanging out with, though, were into shooting up. Like many addicts, I had an inward hierarchy of judgment: I would do *that* for drugs, but not *that*. And I would never *ever* shoot up.

Almost everyone who sets up such rules for themselves, I've learned, eventually breaks them. There had been a time I would have never traded sex for money ... until I did. And one night I got angry at the guy I was dating and went over to a friend's place intending to shoot up for the first time. "If you won't do it to me, I'll try to do it myself."

So she did, because that's what *friends* do, right? And I didn't like it, that first time. I freakin' *loved* it. I was immediately and unequivocally hooked.

It was quite the love affair – until I blew every vein in my body. It eventually took me an hour just to find a place to hit. Reality set in when I got a court date, after three years of being out on bail. I anticipated getting off with probation only and time served, but I figured I'd better detox myself so everything would be copacetic. If I showed up high, I was sure I'd land back in jail.

At the time, I was shooting twenty Dilaudids®, a derivative of morphine, an opiate that tricks your brain into thinking it needs more and more of it. Detoxing before court was even worse than my detox in jail. As I mentioned when I was telling you about Skyy, I couldn't walk. Everything went right through me. I don't even remember the first three days. I was sweating constantly, but also cold like you wouldn't believe. I took Suboxone®, a medication used to treat addiction, but took it too early in the process; it made me even sicker. I'd always tried to be thinner, but now my weight plummeted to ninety-five pounds. There are no words to adequately describe how miserable the experience was.

Still reeling from it all, I went to court, barely able to stand beside my lawyer when the time came. I hung on to the table in front of me for balance. I was a complete mess, too sick to do my hair or makeup or even care. Even my lawyer asked me if I was okay.

I stood there, the epitome of a junkie, but by some miracle, some wrinkle in the universe, the judge decided that I was an intelligent young lady. No one was more surprised than I, but all I could think was, *Thank you, God.* I got off with probation, as planned, but celebrating this small victory would have to wait. I needed to get out the hell out of there and get back to my sickbed.

Spiritual Awakening

Once I was on probation and got an apartment, I got into a magical car accident.

A little explanation: The car accident itself wasn't magical, but I had had the most intense intuition concerning it. I planned to go to Miami for the final day of the Winter Music Conference. This is an annual event, a weeklong electronic music bonanza where thousands of people go to dance and party. Definitely my kind of thing.

But from the beginning, my gut, my intuition, my spirit, whatever you want to call it – tried to dissuade me. There were plenty of signs. I had severe anxiety over trivial things; I couldn't even decide what to wear. The air conditioning in my apartment wasn't working. When I dropped Skyy off to a friend, the dog completely freaked out – something she never did. I planned to ride with my friend Michelle and her husband, but that got screwed up too. I would have to follow behind them in my car. Considering that I had no tread on one of my tires, I knew this wasn't the safest solution.

I hadn't learned to trust the universe at that time, though. I didn't see the signs or trust my intuition. I thought that all of the red flags flying in my face were disconnected, random events. All the changes, my dog, the anxiety – I paid no attention. All the way to Miami, the heavens poured down rain as if trying to give me one last chance to turn around and go home. I could feel that bald tire spinning, not connecting with the road as it should, but I ignored it because *I wasn't connected to myself* yet.

Somehow I made it to Miami. When we arrived at the couple's hotel we had a drink there before leaving for the venue. People wait all year long to get tickets for this conference, but although my friends had tickets, I did not. I might be waiting in line for hours only to be denied; it didn't seem fair to delay their fun. "Go on in without me," I told Michelle.

Across the street, I saw two guys I knew standing outside of what was, by comparison, a pretty rank club, but I reasoned that a rank club would be better than standing in line for nothing. We partied awhile, danced. Fortunately, I didn't have a lot to drink. They had been at a pool party the whole day, so they weren't wanting a late night anyway. Before we split up, I asked them to drive me to my car, which wasn't out of their way at all, it turned out. They were staying at the same hotel as Michelle and her husband, where I'd parked my car.

Never one for boundaries, I almost didn't put my seat belt on that night. Thank God I did. Just as we approached our exit, BOOM! We crashed into the median. The whole front of the car was smashed in. We were all in shock, and shock is something else, let me tell you. I had no idea at the time that I had a broken foot, broken knee, and separated clavicle.

I didn't know because I was walking. I walked with a broken foot and knee, thinking I was perfectly fine. I'd been in the backseat, so you would think the guys up front would have been more banged up. They were hurt, but as it turned out, their injuries were minor compared to mine.

When the tow truck arrived, I got a ride to my car. One of my friends came along. Only when we got to my car did I realized I couldn't walk. My friend had to help me out of the truck and to my car. Safely inside, the pain kicked in suddenly. I knew I'd never make it if I tried to drive. Thankfully, Michelle and her husband were back at the hotel by then, and answered my call. He came down and helped me back to their room, where Michelle, an orthopedic physical therapist, diagnosed the breaks.

"No, you're wrong!" I insisted. "I just sprained my ankle or something." The minute I saw my reflection in the bathroom mirror, however, I freaked out. A broken clavicle is not a pretty sight.

My friends were adamant: I needed to go to the hospital. "Just let me sleep!" I begged, but not even five minutes of laying on the couch was enough to convince me; Michelle called 9-1-1.

The ambulance took me to a Miami hospital, of course, but when my mother arrived from Port St. Lucie, she asked that I be transferred closer to her home, two hours away. The ride was hell. Three days in the hospital, confined to a wheel chair for three months. Shoulder surgery. The hits just kept on coming. And coming: During the month following the accident, three of my friends died. Three. It was too much to take.

But the accident was magic, remember? Now I see that all of it was necessary for me to get to the good stuff.

The first night out of the hospital, I had an out of body experience at my mom's house that was mind blowing. It changed my life, turned it upside down and inside out. The source in my experience, my guide, was in female form. She had several messages to deliver. I had a gift, she said, that I needed to use to help others. "Your car accident happened for a reason." A few of the messages, I no longer remember. Someone I can only describe as an angel then escorted me back to my body.

Afterward, I slept. When I woke up, I immediately asked Mom for a notebook so that I could jot it down. It was all so real. And so absurd, when I thought about it. What did it mean?

My research began. Having had an out of body experience myself, I wanted to learn everything I could about them. They occur often enough that there's even an acronym: OBE. I watched YouTube videos on spirituality, listened to binaural beats and learned about sound wave therapy. I studied meditation. Whereas I had been all over the place inwardly, before the experience, after it I was suddenly focused.

It was a magical time for me. Light seemed to flood in. Everything in my life became involved, connected in synchronicity. It was like a spiritual game of connect the dots. My mom took me, still in a wheelchair, to meditation groups. People were shocked at my positivity and obvious happiness. At one session, I received a blessing from a woman I had connected with in particular; she said she had some messages for me. Oddly enough (yet not odd at all) her messages mirrored those of my OBE's source: *The accident happened for a reason. You have a gift and need to use it to help others.* And so on.

During this time of physical and spiritual healing, my mom took me for a reiki session. Reiki is a form of alternative medicine also referred to as energy healing. "Universal energy" is transferred from the hands of the practitioner into the body of the client. When I arrived for my first session, the lady and I became so excited; both of us felt that we already knew each other. For the *third* time, the messages were repeated. As the reiki practitioner used the heel of her hands to gently impart energy, sometimes holding them above my skin, she spoke: *The accident happened for a reason. You have a gift that you must use to help others.*

The universe had my undivided attention.

Everything took on a magical quality during the next three months. Tons of research behind me, I felt filled to the brim with knowledge. I came to the conclusion that I'm both an indigo child and an empath, research backing up my personal life experiences. I had lived with the fog for so long. Now, the sun was beginning to break through.

Have you ever looked through the lens of the camera as it took a second for the scene to come into focus? That's what I felt had happened, although it had taken my entire life to reach this point. I realized that in complete opposition to the lies I had believed, I had purpose. Things had happened for a purpose.

Signs had come, even in childhood, but now I recognized them for what they were. I gave them my attention. I was in touch with both my physical self and the natural world in a new and exhilarating way. Even more profoundly, I connected with the deeper reality of the great beyond, the supernatural, the spirit realm. Meditating every day, I developed the ability to see auras around others, colors of different energies.

I mentioned earlier that three friends died within the first month of my accident. What was the hidden purpose there? I took it as a warning. How easy it would have been for me to have died on the road to Miami, or when we crashed into the median. I couldn't attend my friends' funerals at the time because of my injuries, but I felt a connection to them as I meditated.

It was euphoric. Every day I received so many signs, it's like they were waiting for me around each corner. I would see heart shaped clouds in the clouds. Rainbows appeared out of nowhere. Butterflies flew up to me and wouldn't leave my side. At home, the power would glitch and instead of seeing an inconvenience, I recognized it as a sign.

I decided that when I was able to get around again, I wanted to train to be a deeksha giver, a giver of blessings, someone who transfers divine energy to others. I had awakened to so much truth because of a blessing through the messages from my OBE guide, later emphasized by others, I wanted to bless others.

What was involved in becoming a deeksha giver? During my research, I had come across information about "oneness awareness"; I attended a two-day workshop that was intensely informational. I became a blessing giver, then went a step further soon after, becoming what is known as a golden orb deeksha giver.

Deeksha givers impart blessings through their hands. Golden orb deeksha givers bless straight through the heart. My mentors and trainers taught me that my blessings were strong, but this was not surprising, as I knew by now that my purpose on earth was to heal. By the way, it is customary for students to travel to India in order to become golden orb deeksha giver, but I was born (reborn) in a time when India could come to me via a TV monitor. All has happened as it should happen, even in that regard.

Hospital Stay(s) and my Heart

Having an out of body experience and being spiritually strengthened, then becoming a golden orb deeksha giver – you might think that now my life was set. All would be happiness and light,

Well. Not exactly.

Let's fast forward to my first open heart surgery. That's right, my *first*. At age twenty-eight.

I had been out the whole weekend before I started feeling ill. It felt like there was a giant lump in my throat; I had a fever. My energy was so low, I couldn't even walk Skyy, my precious and constant companion. It was difficult to even breathe.

I could usually depend on Mom at such times, except now she was on a cruise, out of the country. Talking to her by phone was helpful, but it just wasn't the same. In my mind I figured it was just the flu. When I didn't get better, though, my mother advised me to see a doctor. And when my dad came to see me, he took one look and said he was taking me to the hospital.

Unfortunately, the doctor at the hospital assumed it was the flu as well. He sent me home, no better than when I'd arrived and getting worse with each passing hour. Soon I was bad enough that my father called 9-1-1. An infection in my bloodstream was the culprit, in addition to pneumonia.

So, a really *really* bad case of the flu – that was my understanding at the time. I was put on IV antibiotics, expecting to feel better soon. The doctor finally explained to me that I actually had endocarditis, a bacterial infection in the inner lining of the heart chambers and valves. Imagine lying in bed, convinced you "just" have the flu, only to find out that you have heart issues.

At first, I was terrified. For a moment, all my training and research, all the blessings spoken over me, *everything* – it all was gone. I became so exasperated that I finally asked the doctor to stop talking, to explain the details to my parents. I just couldn't hear any more. As I lay there, though, the connection returned. It was like being deep in the ocean. Overhead, the waves swirled and the wind howled. I was deep enough that the turmoil could not affect me. I would be okay. I knew it, whether anyone else did or not.

It was too late to fight the infection with IV antibiotics alone, however. A veritable battery of tests was performed. My back was cut open to release fluid that had built up. The doctors tried for weeks, but now surgery was necessary to repair my heart's tricuspid valve. I hadn't even known I *had* such a thing, and now I would have open heart surgery to repair it. Everyone was amazed that I could remain positive, attributing it to my bravery. The truth is, I was simply certain of a good outcome. When you know, *you know*.

When I came out of surgery I was completely delusional, convinced I was at a party. Everyone I spotted through the haze was having a blast while I lay there with a tube down my throat. Thank you, anesthesia! The nurses asked questions to determine if it was okay to remove the tube, but I kept gagging in misery. Finally the tube was removed.

If you've never had open heart surgery you may not realize the incredible post-surgery challenges. You have to learn how to live again, how to walk again with a walker.

You've had your chest cracked open and it hurts. Badly. *Everything* is difficult. The doctors told me that my infection had been caused by years of taking drugs. If I used again I would die.

I stayed positive, however, determining to be a blessing to those around me, working hard to get better so that I could continue to fulfill my purpose in life. There was something nagging me, though, a whisper that this wouldn't be my last battle. I hoped that this was not a sign, *not* a message. I hoped that this time, the whisper meant nothing.

Only a few months later, I felt sick again. It was only sporadic, but I decided not to take a chance. The last time I had waited too long; now I went to my cardiologist quickly, who ordered blood work. When I went to the hospital the next day for blood work, I had no idea that I'd be back inside those walls within twenty-four hours.

By that night I was much worse, feverish, completely out of sorts. My symptoms only increased by the morning, which happened to be Friday the 13th. I had a difficult time getting out of bed; I could barely take Skyy outside to do her business. Something was seriously wrong again. Mom, who was retired and traveling a lot, was out of the country again. I called 9-1-1. Soon I was back at the all-too-familiar emergency room.

Mom flew back from Jamaica that evening to be with me. I was grateful, but also a little annoyed. I had told her not to leave, I reminded her; I had had one of my "feelings" that something would happen. It felt like a pattern was emerging: Mom leaves, I get sick. A whisper of fog descended.

My fever was 103° despite taking four aspirins that morning. After several tests it was determined that I had developed a staph infection in my bloodstream. I wanted to believe that that was all that was wrong, but the sense of déjà vu was strong. They pumped me with antibiotics, no easy task with a former addict. I had blown so many veins, that starting an IV line was much more difficult. At one point, the IV solution was pumped directly into my arm, missing a vein completely. My arm swelled up like a balloon from the resulting inflammation.

The next day I was told that I had pneumonia again, which seemed like good news. No surgery! Intuitively, however, I sensed that something more complicated was going on that the doctors had not yet discovered.

A test showed no growth of any sort on my tricuspid valve that had been surgically repaired. On the third day of my stay, my gut feelings were validated. Endocarditis again. This was bad news, but not surprising. The doctors hadn't mention surgery yet, but in my heart – the organ of everyone's focus at the moment – I knew it was coming.

When a valve test was performed a second time, growth was detected. I would need open heart surgery again. The heart surgeon explained that my best option was for them to replace the previously repaired valve. Upsetting as this was, there wasn't anything else to be done. I was helpless to change the circumstances, and so I accepted it. I would be okay. I would be even better than okay when the nightmare was over.

With the previous surgery, the doctors had waited two weeks, hoping they could fight the infection with antibiotics. This time, they didn't waste a minute. The operation was scheduled for Monday, and the worst part was knowing that I'd wake up with that damn tube down my throat again.

Monday, I was placed on what looked and felt like a human platter. Gooey cold slabs of something were applied to my back. I couldn't wait for the anesthesiologist to put me out, to stop the anxiety that was rising. When the anesthesia airway mask was set in place, I was relieved. You can go anywhere you want while you're on an anesthesia, and I was looking forward to the trip!

When I woke up, though, it was to the same terrible party scene. I was confused again, unable to process the situation accurately. It seemed so unfair! The worst part was that at first, I was awake but unable to move. I couldn't even open my eyes for what *felt* like a good hour or so. It was miserable. I struggled to lift an eyelid or flex a muscle, but my body refused to cooperate.

When I came out of the anesthesia a bit more, my immediate focus was the tube. I couldn't stop gagging. Once again, the nurses had to determine that I could safely breathe on my own. How the hell was I supposed to breathe with a fucking tube down my throat?! The poor nurses finally realized I wasn't going to stop gagging; they had me hold my breath for a final test, after which they mercifully removed the tube. *Ahhhh.*

I was parched to the core. Liquids were not an option, but the ice chips the nurses brought became my new best friends. I couldn't get enough.

Once more, post-surgery helplessness was endured. Someone had to give me a sponge bath. I had a catheter inserted up my hoohah, and chest tubes to drain blood and other fluid from my lungs. Someone re-positioned me often so I wouldn't get bedsores; I was in so much pain, I couldn't move much on my own. And always, the feeling of being watched, monitored carefully in the ICU. I've always wondered whether this contributed to the paranoia that began to build up in me later.

Damn complications. I developed a blood clot that sat stubbornly on my lung, making it very difficult for me to breathe. After a CAT scan was done, a tube was placed to drain the clot which didn't work. The plan was to open me back up through the open heart incision to remove the clot.

A third surgery? Ugh. Pain again. That stupid tube down my throat again. I sucked up all my negative feelings and focused on the positive. Clot removed, I would be able to really start healing. There was no way around it; the process was necessary. The more I cooperated inwardly, the better the outward results.

Back on the platter, I was grateful that this would be a quicker and easier procedure than before. I told myself that *this* time, I wouldn't wake up thinking I was at a party. And I didn't! The tube was every bit as troublesome, but I wasn't confused. The tube was removed more quickly this time and I consumed a ton of ice chips. Getting to chug a few cups of ice water was absolutely thrilling, but as the anesthesia wore off, the pain was also excruciating. From years of opiate addiction, I still had an unusually high tolerance for pain medication. Medicine that would have been great for other patients didn't even touch my discomfort.

And then more news came. The surgery to remove the clot had been successful, but my heart was weakening. It wouldn't be able to beat sufficiently on its own, so a pace maker was necessary. As much as I dreaded another surgery, at least this time, I wouldn't have a tube down my throat! Oh, joy!

I was ready.

The next day, the doctor who would place my pacemaker explained the procedure. He would do it that same day. The anesthesia was so effective that I woke up wonderfully loopy, feeling no pain, talking nonsense, even singing a song – a little embarrassing *now*, but I'm sure they've seen worse.

My recovery began once more. Remember, my sternum had been sawed through twice. My chest had been cut open twice. The pain from those events was so bad that I didn't even notice the residual discomfort from the pacemaker procedure. I couldn't sleep because of the pain even after injections of Dilaudid®, morphine, Percocet®, and more. The nurses couldn't believe it. "Her tolerance to pain meds is insane!" one nurse exclaimed to my mother.

Well, that's what happens when you've been addicted to all that shit, I wanted to tell her. Long after you're clean, your tolerance remains higher than normal. I was in intensive care for close to a week due to the multiple surgeries in a row. When I was moved out, I was given Dilaudid® pills. I had received such high doses of pain meds in ICU, even though they were ineffective, that my body reacted now as if I were detoxing.

So on top of everything else, I felt like crap: restlessness, cold sweats, irritability, discontent. What would help? I asked the doctor to switch me to Percocet®, not as strong. I figured that if I was going to be sick regardless, I might as well get off the heavy stuff as soon as I could. Even then, I felt miserable. Finally, I asked to step down to tramadol, a synthetic opiod.

My body adjusted to the change quickly, and I felt a million times better.

Not long after my chest tubes were removed, I was transferred to the fifth floor, starting to feel like myself again mentally. I was in a double room, but the staff tried to keep me by myself for as long as possible, since I'd be there until the end of December. I was actually okay with the idea of spending the holidays in the hospital.

To pass the time and reinforce positivity, I read inspiring books about the mind and the brain. The first was *Change Your Thoughts, Change Your Life* by Wayne Dyer. This is an incredible read and helped me in many ways. I felt more peaceful and accepting of everyone and everything after I finished it.

I read that we forgive in measure, as we are able. Now I was able to forgive those who had hurt me at a deeper level, to see the good in all. It wasn't that Dyer's words were dramatically new to me but seeing things from his perspective hit me hard, in a good way, validating my thinking.

Eventually an older woman was moved into my room who moaned all night. I felt bad for her, but I was still quite sick, needing quiet in order to rest and heal. The next day she screamed the whole day. Literally. It was agonizing to hear her pain like that, helpless to alleviate it. I didn't judge her but it was awkward, affecting my peace. When my mom visited that day, we spent most of our time sitting at the end of the hall by the elevator because in the shared room, we couldn't hear ourselves talk over the screaming.

Every hospital has special codes they can call as needed; the staff there eventually called a "code indigo" for rapid response (ironically, to an indigo child like me). I wasn't allowed back into the room at that time. Thankfully, I was moved to a private room on the eight floor to better accommodate my long term needs. A cozy little room on the top floor – Mom and I laughed that it was almost like having a penthouse apartment!

In relative quiet, my healing progressed more quickly. Spiritually, I felt reawakened. Despite my circumstances, I felt more positive and accepting than ever. The light was dispelling the fog more often than not. I felt unconditional love toward others in a deeper way than I'd ever experienced. My heart had been opened physically – twice – and now it felt spiritually and emotionally open, with love pouring from the inside out.

One major benefit of my trials and tribulations was the wonderful relationship I began to enjoy with my father. Coincidentally (if I believed in coincidences, which I did not) we had had a terrible argument the day before I was admitted to the hospital. He had felt horrible when he found out about the surgery; no one knew what to expect. "I don't think she'll ever speak to me again," he said to Mom. When she told me what he'd said, I have to admit that I wasn't sure I would either.

After my surgery, though, there was a texted apology from my father waiting on my phone. This was a shock; my father *always* had problems admitting he was wrong. Fearing for my life had been a bit of a wake-up call for him. I texted back a simple message: *I love you. I want to see you!*

The next day he was at my bedside. We cried and hugged, and I felt a love for him unlike I had ever felt. I had come a long way on my spiritual journey, but I realized that I had kept my father in a separate place, all to himself. I had forgiven others, but not him.

Finally letting go of my resentment towards him because of the past, I made a conscious decision to separate his *behavior* from his *person*. His anger issues might always remain, but I would focus on who he was at other times. When he was in a good mood, he was absolutely wonderful, a delight to be around. I chose to focus on that.

I no longer saw anger and personality issues as *part* of him. Diagnosis of bipolar disorder or whatever label he was given, I believed that he could learn, in time, to manage his anger when he was ready to open his mind. Thankfully, this is exactly what happened. Where he used to laugh at my ideas on spirituality, he now listens. He learns. He can see with his own eyes the inspiration my experiences have brought to others, and he has finally taken the time and trouble to get to know his daughter for exactly who I am. This was never the case as I was growing up, when I was expected to be someone I was not. And perhaps I also expected *him* to be someone he was not.

What a blessing. After reading one of my books about thoughts, the brain, and the mind, he began to do something that blew my mind: He started to meditate. My dad! Meditating! He's Jewish, but although the Torah speaks of meditation many times, he had always turned up his nose at the idea.

Today when my father visits me, he joins me in meditation and he *enjoys* it – but who wouldn't? Meditation heals and stills the mind, exactly what he has needed for so long. Historically, he gets overly excited about small things, overreacts to things that are not worth getting worked up about. It has been both shocking and delightful to see our relationship grow, flourishing into a real friendship.

Because I chose to let go of the hurt and bitterness where my father was concerned, today I can talk to him freely, no longer feeling the need to hide my spirituality from him in order to avoid conflict. And for his part, he realizes that my gifts are valid because he has witnessed firsthand their positive effect on others. We have exchanged such sweet, kind words to each other, all the angry accusations are forgotten. Sometimes, he even asks for my advice. This is nothing short of miraculous.

It is a delight to see this man continue to change in a positive way, and it is my hope that he makes consistent, small changes as he learns more, so that his life can be the best possible. If I could change *my* ways, *my* thoughts, *my* depression, surely others can. Surely *he* can.

A New Life, a New Lifestyle

The nurses were shocked by my positive attitude and outlook. I believed that it was truly my last chance. My infectious disease doctor told me that I was very lucky. Many people would not have survived what I had been through. "If there is a next time – which there won't be – there would be nothing we could do."

My last chance. That concept inspired me to stay clean and maintain a healthy lifestyle. This included staying away from toxic people who could lead me to harmful behaviors. I had seen, too many times, friends in recovery slip into their old lifestyles. It's easy to do because addictive thinking may remain after addictive behavior ends. It's all about *now*, without thinking of possible outcomes.

I knew that it was crucial for me to surround myself with supportive people who were aware of my situation and genuinely wanted the best for me. Using drugs again, even a little bit, would be devastating.

We each have needs. When we have trained our minds and our bodies to meet those needs through drugs, we must find alternatives. Like the saying goes, *reality is for people who can't handle drugs.* My reality was and is my spirituality, which includes healing, meditation groups and healing circles, automatic writing, kundalini yoga, shamanism, meditation, shamanic journeys, the mind machine (a machine with different settings which put out different frequencies, and color track glasses to wear during the session), out of body techniques, lucid dreaming techniques, binaural beats, and listening to inspiring spiritual teachers. Bear in mind, this took *years* of research and development. Steady, small steps of learning. I would delve into one aspect of spirituality and hear of another, and so it went.

It was my pleasure to attend two amazing workshops at The Monroe Institute in Virginia, whose vision is the global awakening of humanity. It is sometimes called TMI, which is the opposite of the texting acronym for Too Much

Information! At *this* TMI, you are always seeking more information, expanding the consciousness.

The first workshop I attended was called OBE Intensive, dealing, of course, with out of body experiences and the different methods and techniques to get out of body. The next was Destination Higher Self, focusing on death, but not as an end – as a shift of consciousness.

Those times were instructive and beneficial, but I have found daily activities that meet my needs as well, which I will share with you later.

My relationship with my father was a major positive outcome following my medical ordeal. Another was that I finally came out as gay. Immediately, a weight lifted off my shoulders. It was such a relief after so many years wondering about my sexuality. I wanted to scream, shout, and let it *all* out. It took time, and I did it my way, but oh, what a happy day.

A Setback of Sorts

Life is never all sweetness and light, of course. Challenges present themselves. "Shit happens."

A particularly appalling event occurred after my heart surgeries. My phone and computers were hacked, which led to my also being stalked. Here I was, trying to recover from heart surgery, and I had to deal with all that too? Yikes.

I was on a phone plan with another person at the time, someone I obviously didn't know well enough before letting him into my life. He showed signs of being a narcissist and a sociopath; worse, he was obsessed with me. He was also the only person who could have hacked my phone. A black hat hacker is someone who violates another's cybersecurity for personal reasons – not to make money, just to be mean; this guy was every *ounce* a black hat hacker. Every replacement phone I got off of his plan, hoping the problem would resolve, was also hacked.

My apartment was also broken into several times. My computer was destroyed, with all of my data, documentation, and modeling pictures – gone. I called the police, but there was nothing they could do. Cars followed me and would sit across the street from where I lived to watch me.

My parents thought it was unreal, that I was crazy – so much so that they Baker Acted me several times, an involuntary commitment to a mental health facility. I felt like I was living in a smart city, where every bit and byte of information was spread throughout the world. I wasn't going insane, regardless of appearances, but the whole situation was insane.

I was afraid to leave my apartment. And I'm not talking about for a few days, or a few weeks. For years, I was afraid to step out of the house. Eventually, my mom picked me up and moved me to her house. That was a more comfortable arrangement, but things that should not have been happening continued after the move.

I was definitely being watched. The guy who had hacked me was former military; perhaps he had connections with the government. I couldn't figure out his motives, other than to make my life miserable. And he was doing a great job.

My life was once again spiraling out of control. Everything seemed to be a conspiracy against me. I found alarming papers in my mother's files. Was she in on everything? When I accused her, she was not happy. Instead, she was sure that I was losing my mind.

My mom didn't really want to help, I thought. When I wanted to get a lawyer, she balked – more proof she was involved! I was super paranoid; everywhere I looked, I envisioned some sinister plot against me. Not only was my mom against me, all of her friends were, too. They talked and laughed about me when they were together, I was sure. Overwhelmed by my accusations and rantings, Mom yelled that she didn't want to hear it. Who would?

The best solution seemed to be setting me up in my own place. Instead of seeing this as a generous gift or a blessing, I was convinced that it was all a set-up: *Mom is trying to kill me.*

Of course she wasn't. And her friends weren't out to get me. There was no government conspiracy to ruin my life. Our bodies are divinely created orchestras, but when the horn section is out of tune, the discord is horrible! In my case, PMDD was once again wreaking havoc.

The fog wanted to control me again, as well.

We finally found a hormone doctor that tested me thoroughly enough to discover that my hormones were all out of whack. My estrogen levels were completely backwards, explaining why I was incredibly tired in the mornings but had higher energy, if I had any at all, at night. Most bodies naturally produce the hormone dehydroepiandrosterone, or DHEA, in the adrenal gland. My body did not get the memo, apparently.

I began DHEA supplements along with vitamin C, magnesium, and others. "Magically," my hormones lined up. Give the body what it needs, and it's remarkable how well it does. Not only do I no longer suffer from PMDD. I barely have PMS.! I feel exceptional all the time. I'm so grateful for that doctor.

It took time for my body to come into balance. During this adjustment period, I developed a terrible rash on my face, neck, chest, and back. It looked like pimples. Lots and lots of pimples. Medicine prescribed by a dermatologist was not effective. A biopsy determined that one of my medications was the culprit. I immediately stopped taking it, of course, but it took a good (bad) six weeks for the rash to clear. My hormones were in flux, I changed medications. I used various creams and washes. Finally, my skin cleared. Another reason for thanks.

During the process of getting my hormones adjusted hormonally ... so, not out of the woods yet, so to speak ... we found a beautiful house for me. I loved it, but I had been through a hell of a lot. I was terrified still, paranoid still, not entirely sure my mother wasn't out to get me. My "stalker" returned, only he wasn't quiet any more. I would hear someone stomping around in the attic. It was horrifying. I was sure someone had a gun up there and was going to shoot through the ceiling and kill me.

I knew I needed help. I reached out to some of the available services, but everyone seemed to think that I was crazy. I wasn't. I knew what I was going through and I knew what was real and what was not. I would play it over and over again in my head, what was happening, what was going to happen next. Skyy would look up at a particular area of the ceiling and I would think, *That must be where they are.* I would run to another part of the house.

Scared and paranoid as hell, I couldn't take it anymore. I packed my bags and headed to my friend Will's house.

It only took a few days for Will's true colors to show, however. Soon after I started crashing at his place, I was getting ready to go with him to a crystal shop. Girls generally take a little more time than guys to get ready, and at the time my rash was still in full force. Will flipped out that it was taking me so long. He stormed out, shouting that the girls at the shop were leaving town and he had to get there. This was the first I'd heard of any time constraints. "So let's go!" I said.

When someone has baggage and they get angry at you, they draw from that baggage. You get the blame for everything. Will definitely had baggage. He threw a fit and walked down to the beach alone, so rude that I gave up following him. "You're just like my mother and sister!" he shouted. Wow. I didn't even know his mother and sister; he was making no sense at all. It occurred to me that he had some family issues to sort out. I had my own problems at the time, but I had been nothing but sweet to him, grateful for a place to stay so that I would feel safe.

My birthday came soon after, what should have been a delightful respite from all the stress of recent months. What actually transpired was very strange. We were going to go for coffee, and I asked him if this time, I could take my time getting ready. It was my birthday; I wanted to look my best. He should have just said no, but he agreed. When I was finally ready, I found him outside, gardening. *He* wasn't ready to go.

Alrighty then. I walked back inside to wait.

Not even a minute later, he came in and asked if I was ready! When I said he'd just told me he was in the middle of something, and asked if he was upset about something, he flipped out again, driving off in his van. I sat outside, trying to regain some balance in the open air. Will wasn't gone long, but when he got back, he locked me out of his house. It made no sense at all, especially on my birthday. I didn't even have all of my belongings from his house. The overreaction, frankly, reminded me of my dad's bad times.

You think you know a person, until an entirely different side is shown. I drove back to my house, immediately aware that I was being followed. When I pulled into parking lots, the same cars pulled in with me, every time. I wrote down license plate numbers when I could.

Will had upset me, but this was just creepy. I didn't know where to go or what to do, so I stopped several times in big shopping centers. Skyy was with me, so I walked her, hanging out, killing time. Back at the house finally, I called my mom. She'd been texting me all day, but I was so paranoid, I had ignored her. "Do you want to get together?" I asked. I had a weird feeling she might be setting me up though, and said as much.

My mother promised me that she wasn't setting me up, but as soon as I got to her neighborhood, police cars surrounded me. Officers literally pulled me out of my car and threw me on the ground. That may have been proper procedure but it felt rude; I would have gotten out of the car peacefully, had they had the courtesy to ask. Who knows what they had been told, though?

My chest was in pain all the time, no matter what I did, a carryover from the surgeries. Getting thrown around did not help ease the situation. In the scuffle, I lost one of my shoes. It was upsetting on so many levels. *Happy birthday, love Mom.* Thrown into the back of the cop car, Baker Acted again. She had lied to me. I felt completely betrayed.

You might think that all of this would have a negative, long-lasting effect on me. The opposite was true. When I got out, I went home to a place of serenity. The attic was quiet. Cars were no longer following me. The hacking eased up. I learned that I had gotten approved for Supplemental Security Income from the government.

There was no logical explanation for it all, neither the bad nor the good. Apparently it took that much time for my hormones to adjust, and the injection that they gave me in the hospital also seemed to make me calmer, because I now felt safe with no paranoia or feelings of scarcity, something else I had struggled with. My mom and I took a test that helped immensely. There were other factors involved in my healing and transformation that I will share in part two, but what a relief to be living a happy and free life again. I was back to myself for good this time, happy and grateful all the time.

Even during this last ordeal, though, I tried to stay positive. Admittedly, it was very difficult. My nerves would be shot, now and then, to the point that I felt like giving up completely. But I didn't. I was too strong for that. The universe never let me forget that.

Mom

Throughout my life, my mom and I had a rough, erratic relationship. On the one hand, I felt like she was always nagging me and never had my back when I was a child. I needed her to be on my side when there was trouble with my father. I tried to forgive her for all of this, but there was always something blocking my way.

On the other hand, there were times when we got along wonderfully well, laughing together, and going places. Mom helped me with my schoolwork, supported me in all my school activities, and took me along on trips. She offered to listen as I shared my problems; she tried to guide me, despite the fact that I often didn't want to take anyone's advice.

When things were good between us, though, something would always happen to drive the wedge between us again.

When the hacking and stalking started, I got *really* upset. Things were bad enough without feeling that no one was on my side.

Not knowing what else to do, my mother kept Baker Acting me, which I felt was not the right way to go with the situation. I moved in with her because I had to get away from the place I had been living, but things got even worse. I started to believe, with all the smart equipment she had and all the files I found in her home, that she was out to get me, that she was in on the whole thing.

Paranoia is a powerful, negative force. I would break down and cry, begging Mom to explain why she was doing this to me. When she told me, over and over, that she only wanted to help, that she wasn't out to get me at all, I was too broken to believe her.

There was only one way to find out the truth. My therapist suggested a test called the MMPI, the Minnesota Multiphasic Personality Inventory.

It's a psychological test that assesses adults, screening for personality and psychosocial disorders. As the test was explained, it sounded as though it was just what we needed. It would conclusively show that a person was a narcissist or a sociopath; an empath or sensitive. I don't know how it works, exactly, but it sounded right. Understand – I didn't want to take the test alone; I wanted Mom to, as well!

If the test proved Mom was not a narcissist or sociopath, I could trust her again. By then, I had moved into my own home; our relationship had already improved slightly. The test would serve to galvanize the truth.

So we both took the test. A few weeks later, my therapist shared the shocking results. My mother was *none* of the horrible things I had suspected. My brain had been so twisted from all the trauma I had encountered, I had accused her wrongly. The hormonal imbalance, past addiction, surgeries – all of that had factored in, creating a perfect storm of paranoid behavior. Now I was free to be who I actually was again, a daughter who loved her mother.

Besides the fact that we tested as complete personality opposites, there was nothing negative revealed. Our relationship improved greatly. I begged for her forgiveness – forgiveness is so much more powerful than paranoia! I had been horrible to Mom, but she forgave me. She was so happy to have her daughter – and her daughter's trust – back.

We now have the most sensational relationship I could imagine. I can't get enough of my mom! I see her whenever I can and we are basically best friends. I have the best time when I'm with her, and she would say the same about the times she's with me. Our relationship is completely and totally healed. We love each other's company, working on ways to be there for each other. Since we *are* such opposite personalities, there is a learning curve on both sides, but I love my mother more than anything in the world. I would do absolutely anything for her, and I know for a fact that she would do the same for me.

To go from distrust, anxiety, fear, anger – to this, with both of my parents? Amazing.

Part Two: Healing

Part One took you through my life, my journey. Despite the challenges and trauma, I emerged a healthy, whole person. At any given moment, if you had seen me, you might not have thought I was healthy in *that* moment, but everything was at work, unseen. As I journeyed, I learned more and more about what I needed to do for myself. Now, I continue to do these things to grow further, and to maintain my health and wholeness.

In Part Two, I want to share with you the ways that I healed myself, the nuts and bolts of how I came out of the fog into the light. These are universal tools anyone can develop; I don't have the monopoly on them! It took hard work and determination, and, I admit, some of the methods may not be for you. But I encourage you to approach each section with an open mind, and give things a try. It won't take long for you to know what works for you, and what does not. The point is, though, that *anyone can heal*. There are strategies that work. My hope is that by sharing what works for me, your own coping skills and spiritual journey will be enhanced.

Healing through Nature

Nature is healing, giving us peace of mind and wonder. Being immersed in nature brings a euphoria to me like no other. Trees, birds, even individual leaves, are incredibly beautiful. When I am enjoying nature, sometimes I want to cry from the sheer beauty around me. Walking in nature can bring your soul to another level. It is alive and part of us. Surrounded by plants and trees, we feel their warm welcome. We feel at home with a tranquil vibe.

When feeling depressed, try going outside for a while. That sounds so simple, but it can be so effective. Opening yourself to nature can fill your spirit with a golden happiness. Sunshine, the sound of the wind gently blowing – it is truly a beautiful experience. Experiencing nature brings out our inner child; we smile and laugh, feeling nothing but serenity.

And nature is, for the most part, free to enjoy! Walk through a park's alluring trails. Hike into a forest. Walk down the beach and breathe with the rhythms of the waves. It can't hurt, and it definitely can help.

Sometimes I sit outside my house with my eyes closed, simply *being*, feeling the charming breeze, allowing the marvelous sun to beat down upon me, listening to the birds chirping, the leaves rustling. I sit there in awe that such beauty is around me, grateful I can experience it.

In Peru and other countries, shamans immerse themselves in nature every day, every night.They also use plants as medicines to cure people. I believe in this 100 percent. Some plant medicines enable people to go on incredible inner journeys, during which they find out who they are, healing themselves. These medicines have been around for *thousands* of years. These experiences are taken very seriously in those cultures, ceremonies and rituals that are sacred.

In our culture, do we take enough time to recognize the healing power of nature? I think we need to actively set aside more time to appreciate the priceless gifts in nature that are all around us, but which are too frequently ignored.

Healing by "Emptying the Garbage"

Sometimes we are conditioned to think of crying as a sign of weakness. It's actually *super* healthy to cry. Despite what others may say, humans are *supposed* to feel. That's why our emotions are called *feelings*. When you hold emotions in or stuff them down, you only have more junk building up inside, more work to do on yourself in the future. There is great benefit to, once in a while, allowing ourselves to have a nice long crying session. Get everything out! Yell and scream. Do whatever you feel like doing. This is called releasing. It's like emptying the garbage can when it's full.

Emotions have a way of building, building, building – we need to empty, to release, or we will explode. I cry easily, usually right when something happens. I don't care what people think. I get my emotions out right there and then. That way, when I actively "empty my garbage can," I only have a small amount to empty.

Some of you have always tried to be "big and bad." You hold it all in because you think it's not okay to cry in front of people. Once in a while, when you're alone, give yourself permission to spill your guts, get it all out. And I do mean all. Yell at whomever you feel like yelling – you're alone; no one else will hear you. Scream at the top of your lungs. Punch your pillow a million times. Just get it out. You will feel ten times lighter after you "empty the garbage." All the negative energy you were holding onto has left! It's gone!

Next, begin the work of *avoiding* that build up. Experience emotion in the moment, right when it comes. That way, there's less to empty. Of course, you don't have to do it that way – you can fill up that "garbage can" to the brim again before you release it all at once; it's your choice. I encourage you to use the garbage can trick, though, because it works.

You won't necessarily cry, either. When the overwhelming emotion is anger, get a pillow and beat the crap out of it; hang a punching bag out in the garage. Whatever the method, keep emptying the "can" and then – this is important, too! – filling it back up with love. There will

103

Sasha Skyy

be much more room for love after you get the contaminated crap out. The whole purpose of releasing the negative is to make room for, and hold on to, the positive: Love.

Healing through Animals

My dog Skyy came into my life for healing purposes. She is the most amazing and wonderful dog, and we are connected on a spiritual level. She had been abused when a friend found her in the road years ago and gave her to me. She healed me; I healed her. We have an unbreakable bond. I also believe that this wasn't our first meeting, that she has been with me before, in other lifetimes. We connect and speak to each other through our eyes.

I also get strong signs from spirits through her. I always know if I've received a sign I've asked for when Skyy shows or tells me. She is unbelievably intelligent, obedient, and caring. She is also gifted intuitively, knowing when something bad is going to happen. It's uncanny the way she tries to communicate with me. She even knows when I'm getting sick! For example, before both open heart surgeries, she was depressed. I was sick, and Skyy just lay on the couch, as if she were grieving due to my suffering.

Skyy seems to know exactly what's going on, adapting well to new situations. While some dogs are frantic when their masters are away, Skyy is not – except for before the ill-fated Miami trip, when she was trying to stop me from going. She knows that I will be back.

Animals are here to help humans heal. They try so hard, even sacrificing themselves much of the time to get through to people. Sometimes people get the message, yet a lot of the time they miss it altogether.

Let's talk specifically about dogs for a moment. Dogs have already mastered unconditional love and loyalty, qualities we are on earth to develop. If they have already attained to a higher consciousness, why are they here? To be our teachers. As you become more aware of the signs a friendly pup gives you, you become more aware of yourself and what you need to work on in life.

When your dog does something wrong, perhaps leave a puddle of pee in the house, examine your reaction. Are you anxious or worried? Your pup is trying to tell you to be *less* anxious or worried. Whenever they do something, they're trying to show you something about yourself. If a dog acts sad, it's because *you* are sad. They want you to cheer up! Dogs are super smart. My dog Skyy is just like me, sweet-natured and caring. She loves me so much and is always by my side when I need her. She's my shoulder to cry on. My precious love.

We also have spirit animals. I mentioned birds and ducks earlier. My favorite animal is the giraffe, one of my spirit animals, I believe. My other two wild spirit animals are elephants and koala bears. They are gentle animals; I am a gentle person. The elephant is a wise animal; I have a wise old soul. This animal represents a new and improved relationship with the sacred feminine in all of her aspects. The koala bear is a symbol of dreams, intuition, and magic. In the same way, everyone that knows me knows that my intuition is powerful. The koala bear also approaches life with a childlike wonder, much like I do. I have learned to live as child, laughing and having fun because you literally never know when it will be your last second here on earth. As I embrace life, so do koala bears. They spend most of their time in trees; I loved climbing trees as a child. In fact, I still do. If I could live in a tree house, I would.

Ducks and other birds often give me spiritual signs. When I lived in one apartment complex, a flock of ducks followed me around. They were the cutest things! I remember one time they blocked my car from the back so I couldn't leave. I literally had to ask them nicely to move, and then scare them by acting like I was going to back over them just to get them to move. One duck greeted me each morning at the bottom of my stairs when I would come out for a walk. There was a period of time when I would ask for signs from my angels or the archangels, and ducks usually appeared.

A significant sign appeared just before my grandmother passed away. I went outside to walk Skyy and found a duck so shattered that its bones were scattered everywhere. It was a sad thing, but I sensed that the duck represented something more. I ran back into my house and researched dead ducks. Repeatedly, I saw that one possible meaning was that I could lose someone.

The next day my mother called me with the news that my grandmother had passed away. In a small, but tangible way, the universe had prepared me. I had grieved a little for the duck, which made the grief at the news, a bit less severe.

Healing through Meditation

When you meditate, you come into alignment with Source Energy, as in the source of life, sometimes referred to as God. Who wouldn't want to experience and enjoy this blissful feeling? I often hear people say that they don't meditate because they don't know how. Learning to meditate is simple. You just have to be willing to try something new and not give up until you get it. Once you understand how it works, you'll see how simple it is and wonder why you didn't begin sooner.

There are several types of meditation. Guided meditations may be found on YouTube; there are also tons of apps for your phone or tablet. Binaural beats is sound wave therapy in which the right and left ears listen to two slightly different frequency tones, yet perceive the tone as one.

Binaural beats instantly relaxes you, and is known to reduce stress and anxiety while deepening your meditation. Hemi-Sync is a rich source for this, and YouTube also.

Silent meditation can be a bit more challenging. There is no sound, no music; you just sit or lie down in silence. Some people have trouble with this because they haven't learned to quiet their minds. My method is to repeat an affirmation in my head, which gives me something to focus on without being distracted by other thoughts.

How to meditate? I recommend lying down or sitting up with your spine erect. I personally find it easier to lie down. If you're a beginner, however, you might want to begin sitting up because of the tendency to fall asleep. Using headphones with guided meditation is a great starting point. Find a guided fifteen to twenty minute meditation. Guided meditations are helpful for beginners, because you can repeat back every word to yourself. This helps to keep you free from distractions, focusing completely on the meditation itself.

Before you begin, though, relax! Relax each part of your body, one part at a time. Once you begin, stay completely still. Do not move, no matter what. If you get an itch, it will go away. Meditation imparts pure joy, so don't risk ruining that for the sake of scratching an itch! Let it be. That's really the purpose of meditation – to let yourself, and everything else, simply *be*. When the meditation comes to an end you'll feel completely at peace and at one with all things. The weight of the world has lifted, and your divine spirit soars. It's a magical feeling, and one you will learn to protect, to guard, to hold on to.

OBEs (out of body experiences) are a kind of advanced meditation. Experiences vary widely from person to person; I have done it once consciously, discovering what it is like to be one with Source. When my spirit came out of my body, I kept repeating, "Higher self now." Suddenly, I felt myself spinning like a vacuum, shooting through the sky. When I landed, it was in an amazing place where everything was love and light and pure knowing. Pure bliss and ecstasy. The very definition of euphoria. Having taken many trips on drugs, I can tell you that this was *so* much better. A new reality.

Lucid dreaming is related. This has become a focus in my life, although I have yet to master it. I try to remember my dreams and learn from them. While dreaming, we move into another dimension. I love to dream! It's actually one of my favorite things to do. To master lucid dreaming, remaining aware during a dream, is my goal, but things like that can't be rushed. It will take as much time as it takes, which is as it should be.

Healing through Positive Affirmations

I am living proof that you can cure your own depression, because I did it. I cured mine. I have shared that I was an addict – a very bad addict, doing twenty pills a day. That amount of opiates definitely messes with your head, making the brain foggy. Whenever I detoxed, I became very depressed. When I explained to my mom how depressed I was, she encouraged me to change all negative thoughts to positive ones, and then repeat them.

This may have been the first time in my life I listened to my mother's advice! I was so desperate, I would try anything. Every day I told myself that I was happy and healthy. I repeated it so often that I grew to do it without thinking. I did it for a long time. And then one day, *I was happy and healthy.* It was like a switch flipped on. *This shit works!* I thought.

I began doing it with everything. I verbalized what I wanted as if I already had it. Some call this "speaking into existence." Because we are in linear time, our thoughts manifest at a slower pace. Out of our bodies, our thoughts create reality instantaneously; in our bodies, it takes a little longer. The more momentum we give the thought, the faster it comes.

For example; if you want to *find* the love of your life, your affirmation might be,"I've *found* the love of my life." Repeating this will bring you closer to the manifestation. It works! I have had things manifest right before eyes. Words matter. Speaking words of affirmation is unimaginably powerful.

When you think about it, you already know this to be true. A child who grows up hearing "You're stupid. You're just like your father, You'll never amount to anything" will be a different adult than one who grows up hearing "You are special. We're so happy you were born. You can do anything you put your mind to." Don't you often meet people in the former situation and sense their pain?

115

I grew up with negative words from my dad, but I have learned that their power is nothing compared to the power of positive affirmation. Bear in mind, affirmation isn't *pretending* that bad things don't exist. Denial is a serious issue. There comes a time in your life when you must take the "E out of Ego, and let go," as it has been said. You can't positively affirm that you didn't screw up at a certain time, for instance. Put the pride aside and be okay with sincerely apologizing when you're wrong and learning from the mistake you have made. This improves the quality of your life tremendously.

It may sound strange, but I actually love being wrong now. Can you believe that? I have no problem whatsoever admitting my wrongs. There is always a lesson waiting for me to find it; I love learning and gaining knowledge. That's one of the main purposes of this lifetime. We can think of our time here in the physical as a training ground.

Healing through Crystals

Crystals are also a big part of my life. They are powerful, strong, and alive. Holding crystals in your left hand permits their energy to flow through you. I have what is called a fear crystal grid and I kid you not, right when I got it, and began speaking the affirmation that the hacking and stalking would go away, my fear vanished along with the hacking and stalking! I also wrote the affirmation on a piece of paper and put it next to the grid. If you have no frame of reference for things like this, that may seem strange, but you can't argue with experience, and that is what happened with me.

Sometimes I put all of my crystals in a big bowl of cold water, and set the bowl outside to cleanse them in the sun. I also use sage to cleanse them. I hold crystals when I meditate, absorbing their power. My strongest crystals are selenite, crystal ball, and blue apatite. A selenite wand is almost like the magic wands in storybooks; you can feel its power when you pick it up. Placing a selenite wand along the spine can align the chakras, the centers in the body through which energy flows.

I use a crystal ball when I do healing and cleansing on myself and Skyy. It is powerful, bringing harmonious, calming energy to any space. When I use it during meditation it enhances my clairvoyance.

Potent blue apatite helps with meditation, lucid dreaming, and out of body experiences. You can feel its powerful energy while holding it during a meditation. It also has a cleansing influence on one's aura, aiding the development of psychic powers and facilitating oneness with the spiritual world.

Another personal favorite is rose quartz. Sometimes, the stones are heart-shaped; holding one brings a heightened sense of love and peace.

Stones and crystals are incredible, left here on earth to help us heal.

Healing through Coping Mechanisms

It's important to always be in alignment, being aware of ourselves and the world around us, having our chakras in balance. If you get thrown out of alignment, it is important to quickly get balanced again.

A valuable concept is to realize that there are no big deals in life. Literally. No big deals. Even death is just a shift of consciousness. I have learned not to get thrown out of alignment easily, but when I do, coping skills are extremely helpful.

We get out of alignment when we allow something to upset or anger us. We feel out of sync, out of sorts, *bleh*. When this occurs, speak an affirmation supporting the fact that there are no big deals in life (word it however you want, such as "This does not matter," etc.). Take a few deep breaths and sit in silence with your eyes closed for a few minutes until you feel the "click" back into alignment. You may call this getting centered or being mindful. Terminology is not as important as experience.

There are vibrations and auras all around us. A favorite practice of mine is to ask my angels and the archangels to help me clear my aura and raise my vibrations, followed by repeating a mantra of love. I say the word LOVE twenty-one times in groups of threes and fours:

LOVE LOVE LOVE ... LOVE LOVE LOVE LOVE ... LOVE LOVE LOVE ... LOVE LOVE LOVE LOVE ... LOVE LOVE LOVE ... LOVE LOVE LOVE LOVE.

Feel free to borrow this! You will feel uplifted and automatically back in alignment afterwards. Another coping mechanism, if you have the time, is meditation. Even a five minute meditation can bring you back into alignment. Breathing exercises help. Yoga or kundalini yoga do also; the latter incorporates meditation and breathing with poses.

Simply repeating positive affirmations can shift you back into alignment.

Saging is yet another tool in the coping toolbox. Sage can clear the energy and space that you are in. You can sage yourself to deplete any negative energy that is on or near you. I personally sage myself and my home everyday while repeating a mantra.

The word *sage* is associated with a Native American word that means "to heal." Smudge sticks of dried ceremonial white sage may be lit or, if you're sensitive to smoke, sage may be used in a spray bottle. When negativity has invaded your home, workplace, or thoughts, saging is an effective coping mechanism whose roots go back thousands of years.

Saging is easy. You can get it at your local spiritual shop or on-line.

My philosophy is that if it works, why not do it? There is no weakness in using coping mechanisms to help – that is why all of these mechanisms have been created, and brought to our attention.

Healing through a Morning Routine

I have a morning routine which has helped me for years. As soon as I wake up, before I even open my eyes, I smile, telling myself what an incredible day it's going to be. This sets the tone for the rest of the day.

When I get up, I wash my face and then look at my reflection in the mirror. Again I smile and tell myself that I'm beautiful. Right away, I sit down and write a gratitude list with ten to twenty things on it. I just keep writing until my pen stops; this puts me in an automatic state of gratitude, the best state to be in when you first awaken.

Next, I make a mixture of water and apple cider vinegar to drink while I do yoga for ten to thirty minutes. This stretches my muscles and energizes my body. After yoga, I meditate for fifteen to thirty minutes. Saging clears out any negative energy.

Finally, I enjoy cold shower therapy. It doesn't have to be a purely cold shower, but I always include at least thirty seconds of cold water to really wake me up and refresh my pores. While I'm in the shower, I repeat positive affirmations to get *that* momentum going.

You may develop a different routine, but regular repetition has a healing benefit. Combining as many positive techniques as possible, a morning routine can really channel your day in the right direction.

Healing through Art

My first book, *Escape the Ordinary,* contains inspiring quotes and poems. I think of writing as art on a page. I'm making a scrapbook of quotes and poems, arranged in such ways as to enhance their message artistically. I'll discuss this more in the section on automatic writing.

Painting also brings me joy. I like to paint objects, giving them a new life. I've found amazing items in the garbage that I've recreated by painting them. I also paint tables and furniture that I've already had, just about everything in my home. I like to be creative with picture frames, decorating around the picture frame in a way that enhances the beauty of the photograph or painting. The process has a healing effect.

I also enjoy making jewelry and hope to eventually find a market for my earrings. Art keeps me busy and inspired, but maybe one day it will also be a financial help.

I encourage you on your journey to use your creative mind and do creative work. It's soothing and healing. Art can be a major focus in life, and for some it will mean the difference between bitterness and healing. We are born with creativity and talent in different areas; when we experiment, discover, and develop, we expand our consciousness in a profound way. Perhaps you are a poet, or a musician, or a gardener, or a sculptor, or a seamstress. These are all forms of artwork.

Healing through Music

Music heals in so many ways. I personally love what is called *house music,* a form of electronic music. The beat reaches me at a deep level, giving me goosebumps all over. Living in Miami made me a true *house head,* as they say. I got stuck on the fierce beat that comes along with this genre of music. It makes me feel alive and in alignment.

Music can bring back memories to reminisce upon; it's a beautiful form of art. It captures your mind, body, and soul. Your body sways to the rhythm and you feel nothing but in the moment. Some music can make you cry, it's so good.

Music amazes me. I have turntables so I can make my own beats, but lyrics can be just as effective. Lyrics can take your heart and spin it around, a tremendous healing mechanism.

Try it! All by yourself, really listen to the music that moves you. Close your eyes and begin to move freely. No one is around to judge you.

I appreciate all genres of music, because they change your mood in different ways. Immersing yourself in music can bring deep happiness and inner alignment. The more you listen, really listen, to music – the more it will change your life in a positive way.

What is your favorite type of music? Let it capture you! Then change it up – experiment with different genres and see which ones have the most positive effect.

Healing through Automatic Writing

After my physical issues – the car accident and the three heart surgeries – I began having beautiful expressions flow through me, thoughts that just came to mind out of another place, it seemed. Sensing their value, I wrote them down or typed them on my phone or computer. Even though I didn't understand it at the time, I was engaging in what is known as *automatic writing*.

I would do a meditation and afterwords, begin to write. Beautiful poetry and quotes would come through me. I believe spirits were helping me when this happened. It was as if someone was moving my hand for me, like it wasn't actually me writing at all. It was amazing!

This continues to happen to me, as I open myself to it. The words are so meaningful to me at times that I just sit there and stare at the words in front of me. I'm in awe that I wrote them. Automatic writing is a gift, but gifts can be developed. My hand doesn't move itself, forcing me to the computer! But as I make myself available and begin, the words just flow. I am so grateful for this gift, which I believe anyone can experience. Settle your mind and let the words flow!

Healing by Resetting to Your Inner Child

Every day when we wake up, we are completely realigned – or we *can* be. We can choose to erase yesterday, to erase all the days *before* yesterday. We have the opportunity to start fresh, with nothing holding us back.

How can you train yourself to do this? *Look ahead.* Stay in the moment and cherish what you feel, see, hear, and taste *in that moment.* Decide to have a playful day! Invite your inner child to come out and have some fun. No more troubles. No more stress.

You can literally press "reset" and begin your new journey right there. Start another chapter of life, making it positive and fresh. On a daily basis, you can decide to do what you want to do in life.

I know – it sounds too easy, doesn't it? But positivity works. Keep that smile on your face and don't let anyone stop you. Believe the things you want are already there right in front of you, even if you don't see them. Start to manifest them with your courageous momentum. Let that beautiful inner light of yours shine, breaking out, glowing.

Paint the wildest dreams in your head, beginning now, with creative imagination. You create your reality. You are in control of your alignment. The goal is to not throw yourself off when you wake up! That is the optimum time of day to reinforce positivity.

Believe in the new day you choose, and troubles will have less power to bring you down. Nothing can stand in your way as you are empowered.

You can do this every single day. This resets your inner child, the child that has hope and joy in simple things. We wake up in alignment, the perfect time to reset and restart your precious life.

Healing through Twin Flames

I believe that each of us has a twin flame, different from a soul mate. You can have many soul mates. A soul mate can be a friend or a lover, someone who crossed your path and either stays in your life or doesn't, but whose interaction with you teaches you something you were supposed to learn.

In contrast, a twin flame is literally your other half. The yin to your yang. Everyone has one but it is very rare that people find their twins in this lifetime. I have not found mine yet, but I believe that I will. That in itself puts a smile on my face.

Twin flames are actually two souls merging as one. The relationship is often difficult; it may ebb and flow, be "on again, off again." No matter what happens, however, you are drawn back to the person. Because of the oneness with your twin flame, there is a tremendous amount of knowledge you can glean from him or her. A twin flame is like a mirror. Together you are best friends, teachers, and lovers. Twin flames experience a unique synchronicity. I look forward to this experience.

Healing through Signs

Every day I communicate with the archangels, asking them for physical signs because I just love the synchronicity signs bring, the aspect of connecting the dots. Sometimes a beautiful dragonfly stays near me and won't leave me alone, and I know my angels are giving me a sign.

Frequently when I look at the clock. The display reads 11:11 or 1:11. Skyy also shows me when my angels want to reassure me that they are present. She actually tries to talk to me; it's so damn cute, it fills my heart with love.

For a while, I used to find dimes on the ground from my best friend Amy after she passed. Her mom still has tons of dimes that Amy had sent; it was a thing she did. I used to find dimes all the time, but once I realized it was Amy, she must have realized I didn't need them anymore in order to be aware of her presence. She stopped leaving them. I'm grateful for this, because I believe that while she left the dimes for me, she was still attached to the physical. I want her to move along in the afterlife and continue forward in her journey.

Birds are a huge sign for me. I've shared about ducks already. Two cranes regularly visit me; I swear they are the archangels Michael and Gabriel! They are amazing, just standing with me while I talk to them. Usually they talk back, too.

Electricity is often used as a sign in my life. Sometimes I can actually make lights flicker. As an empath, my energy field is larger than usual. One time as I was leaving my neighborhood, each light turned off on buildings as I drove by them. When I returned, each light turned back on as I passed it. True story! It happened two months after my grandmother had passed away, and I had been told that she would be in resting for two months.

I figured she was behind the lights, but I wanted to be sure. So I spoke out to the universe. "If the lights were you, Grandma, make the wind-chime chime." The wind-chime was under a cover, and there was no wind at the time. But it chimed.

Signs can be shocking, but they are magical. Here's the thing: You have to invite your angels and spirit guides to interfere in your life, or they will not. You must give them permission. I do so, because the signs they will send are truly healing and exciting.

Healing through Altered Memory and Energy

There are tons of different healing methods, some of which have been effective in my own life and that I have shared here. The one essential method that I absolutely swear by, because it has had the greatest impact on my own life, is altered memory.

We all have seed thoughts that we have carried since we were children. These seed thoughts continue to affect how we think as adults. They don't go away. If our seed thoughts are negative, we need to alter the memory.

The method that I live by is simple, but effective. Whenever I feel something negative such as sadness or anxiety, I "sit with" the feeling. I tell the feeling, "I'm here with you now, I'm here with you now." Then I ask the feeling if there's anything it wants me to know. Automatically, my subconscious responds. Next I say, "Show me the last time I felt this." From my subconscious, I get a sense of the last time, which could be yesterday, a week ago, a month ago. Next, I say, "Show me the *first* time I felt this feeling."

You must trust your subconscious for this to be effective. Your subconscious will take you back to the very first time you experienced the feeling. You may actually see, in your mind's eye, the first time. You may experience a strong feeling and become aware of its root. Either way, the feeling will most likely connect with your childhood.

At this point, I let myself re-enter the memory so that I can alter it. In the midst of that memory, I make myself as happy a child as possible. I "go up" to the child-me, giving her a hug, telling her that everything is going to be all right.

When you use this method, do whatever you have to do to make the child feel better. Bring angels in. Let the child play and be having fun. You are altering the memory of your inner child and your inner child will thank you for it. This method alters the memory associated with the negative thought or feeling for good. Now, when you feel that feeling again, you will think of the altered memory instead.

Altered memory has been extremely helpful to me, and I hope that you will try it.

Scans are helpful as well. I do scans on myself and also Skyy, to make sure there is no negative energy stuck inside our bodies, entreating the assistance of my angels and the archangels. I scan slowly through each body part while seeking any parts that feel tightness or constraint. If you find discomfort, breathe into it, make a positive affirmation and ask your angels to help you heal and let go of what is causing that discomfort.

Also if Skyy is hurt or I am hurt, there is a way to heal with energy. For example, if my dog hurts her paw, I get the okay from the angels and from my divine first. It is important to connect with them and make sure that they are present to help. I cast a mental fishing pole to hook onto my dog's paw, and virtually coat the paw in whatever color my spiritual helpers tell me to, or whatever color my gut tells me to. Next, I determine where the problem lies, where the pain is, and ask the angels to take it back up with them. Then I "coat" it with protection. When everything has been done that should be done in order to ease Skyy's pain, I bring that mental fishing rod back. I repeat the LOVE mantra, and thank my

139

angels before disconnecting from my divine. This method works with people, too, not just with animals.

Healing through Synchronicity

My life is synchronicity, a series of "connect the dots." Everything leads to something else. I can now connect every event of my life, starting when I was a child, continuing all the way until this very moment. What used to fill me with confusion, anxiety, and pain now makes perfect sense.

Synchronicity is not unique to me. Everyone's life connects perfectly, but not everyone pays attention. Not everyone has learned this truth. *Everything* happens for a reason, both a physical reason and a reason that connects where you were, to where you are, and to where you will be.

Life is like a giant puzzle. I love taking the puzzle pieces, the signs, the events, the clues, and seeing how they all fit perfectly together into the beautiful picture of our life. Our job in this life is to discover that picture.

Sasha Skyy

There is no such thing as coincidence, there is only synchronicity. The more we develop our awareness of synchronicity, the more healed we become, the more alive.

Not the End, but a New Beginning
Staying in the Light

As you can see, my childhood and younger years were quite foggy. I've been through many experiences and could have shared them in such a way as to evoke pity. But, instead, I've tried to share them as lessons which I chose to learn from. Almost always, I chose the positive route. Maybe not at first, but eventually. While I do not celebrate the bad experiences and bad choices that have made up much of my life, I truly celebrate what I have learned from them.

I want to always learn and grow from my experiences, because I believe that that is why we are here: to conquer our mishaps instead of letting them defeat us, to grow from situations we encounter instead of allowing them to destroy us.

No one wants to be neglected or abused or raped or taken advantage of or betrayed. Many people dread spending time in the hospital. No one enjoys injury or disease or surgery. I hit many "bottoms" before I began moving upward consistently. It would have been easy, perhaps, to wallow in my circumstances. Instead I was positive and brave, a choice that inspired others while building my own spirit up.

We are born, and I believe re-born, to expand our consciousness. Every barrier we encounter is an experience to grow from. I cannot emphasize that one truth often enough. Things happen in our lives with our families, with our friends, at the hands of strangers, both because of our own uninformed choices and also because of things completely out of our control. Many things happen *to* us that are in no way our own fault, or which happened when we were too young or unequipped to deal with them.

We must stop blaming ourselves for things that don't belong to us. We must stop taking things so personally. We must stop running and hiding, letting the fog and darkness cover and overwhelm. We can choose to move out of our proverbial comfort zones where we feel safe and out of sight, and *get out there* by starting to do what we truly love.

My prayer for you, my encouragement to you, my hope for you, is this: Step into the light and see yourself shine. You are truly capable of anything you want in life.

This is what I did, against all odds. Through my spiritual awakening, but also through the traumas I experienced, I stepped into the light so that I could shine like the brightest star.

Even if you are in the fog today, my friend, know that you were not born for the fog. That is not your identity. The fog is not your destiny. You, too, have the ability to shine like the star you know, deep down, that you are. Be free. Step into the light, and *stay* in the light.

Thank you for Reading Out of the Fog, into the Light by Sasha Skyy.

Please post a review on Amazon

Escape the Ordinary

Open Your Mind to New Perspectives

SASHA SKYY

Available at all bookstores and online

www.ingramcontent.com/pod-product-compliance
Lightning Source LLC
Chambersburg PA
CBHW031514040426
42445CB00009B/218